Peasants, Agrarian Socialism, and Rural Development in Ethiopia

About the Book and Author

One of the few systematic field surveys undertaken following the 1975 agrarian reform in Ethiopia, this study analyzes the conditions constraining agricultural productivity of peasant farmers in the Arsi region and examines how farmers view peasant and government organizations established to attain agrarian socialism. Based on data generated through interviews with farmers, peasant association leaders, and extension agents, Dr. Dejene argues that the low prices for agricultural products, shortages of consumer goods, and lack of improvements in farming technology are among the major obstacles to increasing output among peasant farmers. The author also explores the government policy of transforming peasant associations into collective farming units, which he finds is supported by only one quarter of the farmers interviewed. His study indicates that peasant institutions could best mobilize labor and resources to generate agricultural surplus and undertake conservation activities that would prevent future famine. Thus the author concludes that present government efforts should emphasize strengthening the cooperative movement rather than establishing collective farming.

Alemneh Dejene is a post-doctoral fellow at the W.E.B. DuBois Institute for Afro-American Research, Harvard University.

Peasants, Agrarian Socialism, and Rural Development in Ethiopia

Alemneh Dejene

Westview Press / Boulder and London

Westview Special Studies on Africa

This Westview softcover edition is printed on acid-free paper and bound in softcovers that carry the highest rating of the National Association of State Textbook Administrators, in consultation with the Association of American Publishers and the Book Manufacturers' Institute.

Copyright © 1987 by Westview Press, Inc.

Published in 1987 in the United States of America by Westview Press, Inc.; Frederick A. Praeger, Publisher; 5500 Central Avenue, Boulder, Colorado 80301

Library of Congress Catalog Card Number: 86-51527
ISBN: 0-8133-7247-X

Composition for this book was provided by the author.
This book was produced without formal editing by the publisher.

Printed and bound in the United States of America

∞ The paper used in this publication meets the requirements of the American National Standard for Permanence of Paper for Printed Library Materials Z39.48-1984.

6   5   4   3   2   1

*To the Ethiopian peasantry, who deserve
a better life and a greater autonomy in
shaping their destiny*

Contents

Foreword

The publicity about the famine in Africa and in Ethiopia touched a common chord in human consciousness. It resulted in an outpouring of compassion from the world community revealing an elevated aspect of humanity that sees starvation in a world of plenty as an affront to everyone. Nevertheless, beyond these noble but piecemeal efforts lies the crucial task of making a concentrated and sustained effort to look into the long-term solution of world hunger.

Dr. Alemneh Dejene's book, *Peasants, Agrarian Socialism, and Rural Development in Ethiopia*, presents thoughtful suggestions that assist in finding such long-term solutions to attain agricultural self-sufficiency in Ethiopia. His study is conducted in Arsi, one of the few surplus producing regions where the Swedish International Development Authority (SIDA) has financed the first integrated rural development projects in Ethiopia. His study is one of the few systematic field surveys conducted after the 1975 Agrarian Reform in Ethiopia. Dr. Dejene has undertaken an exacting task of generating, analyzing, and interpreting original data. He has succeeded in presenting the data in an instructive and insightful way that makes his study valuable for both academicians and practitioners involved in rural development.

Dr. Dejene's study addresses some of the pertinent problems that constrain peasant farmers' production. These problems have also been of concern to SIDA and include insecurity of tenure, inefficiency in the present marketing and distribution system, ineffectiveness of the extension system in disseminating improved innovations to individual households at the village level, and heavy investment in promoting collective forms of production at a stage when most farmers are unaware of the benefits of collective efforts. The findings have national implications since Arsi has been an experimental ground for new ideas and innovations, and farmers in Arsi tend to be more progressive than those in other regions in Ethiopia.

Dr. Dejene suggests that the most viable strategy to overcome these obstacles and increase peasant production is to capture and maximize the potential created by the Agrarian Reform. This potential lies mainly in the peasant institutions, particularly the service cooperatives, which could serve as vehicles to promote the *cooperative movement*, to bring rapid rural development and the gradual social transformation of the rural sector. Moreover, the cooperatives could generate an investable surplus in the peasant sector.

As demonstrated in Arsi, peasant associations and service cooperatives have the capacity to generate a surplus capital through labor and resource mobilization. These peasant institutions have pooled labor to build schools, clinics, and infrastructures, and have undertaken conservation practices that include soil and water management and reforestation to prevent future famine. Service cooperatives are promoting production and income-generating enterprises such as flour mills, dairy farms, and cottage industries. In addition, the majority of service cooperatives have assumed the task of input distribution and credit management formerly carried out by the extension service. They have also shown the potential to have an increased role in crop marketing and distribution of consumer goods, which are presently dominated by government parastatals.

Dr. Dejene's study draws a distinction between the *cooperative movement* and the promotion of collective farming. The latter has been given primacy by the Ethiopian government on the assumption that large-scale collective farming is superior to small-scale farming. As a result, the cooperative movement, by and large, is viewed as a means of transforming peasant farming directly into a collective form of production, i.e., producer cooperatives. Dr. Dejene's caution against this policy is well founded given the present level of subsistence farming, lack of exposure to modern methods by the majority of farmers, and the experience of large-scale agriculture (under the Ministry of State Farms) in Ethiopia.

In all, Dr. Alemneh Dejene's book presents strategies on the issues that adversely affect peasant production. The solution, as he suggests, largely rests on having more faith in, and granting more autonomy to, peasant institutions. This would seem to be a very constructive suggestion for Ethiopian policymakers and outside donor agencies.

Johan Holmberg
Assistant Director General
Swedish International Development Authority
Stockholm, Sweden

Acknowledgments

Numerous people assisted me while I was undertaking this survey research in Ethiopia. The collaboration of extension agents, peasant association leaders, and peasants was vital in generating the data for this research. Mr. Aklu Girgre and Mr. Gizaw Negussie, Vice Ministers in the Ministry of Agriculture, and Mr. Debela Dinka, General Manager of ARDU, were most enthusiastic in supporting this research. I am grateful for their encouragement and support.

The Swedish International Development Authority (SIDA) has contributed significantly towards the successful completion of this research. I have benefited greatly from my continuing discussions with SIDA staff members on issues of agricultural policies in Ethiopia. Chief among them are Mr. Lars Leander, Goran Bergman, and Micheal Stahl. I am also grateful to Mr. Carl Tham, SIDA's Director General, for his encouragement of my research effort.

The W.E.B DuBois Institute for Afro-American Research at Harvard University has also greatly contributed in getting this book ready for publication. I extend my deep appreciation to Professor Nathan I. Huggins, the Director, and Randall Burkett, the Associate Director, who were generous in extending the resources of the Institute to support this as well as my other research activities on Ethiopia.

I have greatly benefited from the encouragement and the support of James McCann, Allan Hoben, and Susan Hoben at the African Studies Center, Boston University; Nigel Roberts and Vincent Ashworth at the World Bank; Assefa Mehretu and Grover Hudson at Michigan State University; Edmund Keller at the University of California, Santa Barbara; and John Harbeson at the City University of New York.

The presence of an inspiring and long time friend in Cambridge, Michael Guillen, a scientist and renaissance man, was extremely valuable in overcoming the difficulties I encountered while undertaking this research. I also extend my appreciation for the assistance of Carrie Noland.

Finally, I would like to thank Ricardo Godoy, Charles Mann, Donald Warrick, Richard Cash, Richard Hook, and the administrative assistants at Harvard Institute for International Development.

The views expressed in this book are my own.

Alemneh Dejene

Chapter 1

Introduction

I. The Nature of the Problem

Sub-Saharan Africa is facing an extraordinary food crisis. For the first time in the history of the United Nations, a meeting was convened in the general assembly to deal specifically with the economic problems of one region - Africa. As the document that is prepared by this special session for seeking more aid put it, "a sick Africa means a sick world and an Africa that remains stagnant or remains perpetually backward economically is a threat to the economy of the world." (1) (See Figure 1)

The optimism of the 1960's concerning the potential for economic development in the newly emerging African countries has been replaced by deep pessimism in the 1980's. Between 1960-70, the annual growth of the gross domestic product (GDP) of Sub-Saharan Africa was 3.8%, its population 2.4% and its *per capita* income 1.4%. But between 1970-81 the annual growth rate of the GDP and *per capita* income of Sub-Saharan Africa had declined to 3.2% and 0.4% respectively, while its population rate was soaring at 2.8%. (2)

Agricultural output *per capita* has declined by about 15% since 1980 in the twenty-four Sub-Saharan African nations classified as the most seriously affected countries by the United Nations Food and Agricultural Organization. Agriculture dominates the economy of these countries, employing over 80% of the population and contributing to over 50% of the GDP. Yet, they rely heavily on food aid and emergency relief to feed over one fifth of the population. (3)

FIGURE 1

<u>Map of Africa</u>

There are many reasons for the dismal agricultural performance in these countries: lack of investment in agriculture, high population growth rate, lack of capital investment to generate growth, lack of incentive to stimulate small farmers' production related to pricing, marketing and supporting services, lack of improvement in crops, livestock and farming practices, lack of infrastructure, drought and ecological degradation, political instability, declining export and prices for commodities, unfavorable terms of trade, shortage of trained manpower and the need for structural reform to induce change. Ethiopia is one of the Sub-Saharan countries most seriously affected by these problems.

Prior to the 1974 Ethiopian Revolution, the most frequently cited problems contributing to Ethiopia's agricultural underdevelopment were structural in nature. These mainly included the *feudal* land tenure system characterized by the absentee landlord, tenancy and land insecurity, and the fatalistic tradition of peasants reinforced by conservative religious institutions, and a feudal structure that was resistant to change and innovation. (4)

The myth about the fatalistic peasant was discarded and most studies attributed Ethiopia's poverty to two causes: (1) the neglect of peasant agriculture and (2) lack of the political will on the part of the imperial government to bring profound political and economic change which would in turn create the necessary conditions to stimulate peasant agricultural production. (5)

The 1974 Ethiopian Revolution overthrew the monarchy and instituted a fundamental structural change in the distribution of wealth and power in the society. It was soon followed by the Agrarian Reform that changed the relationship between the owners and tillers of the land. The Agrarian Reform dealt with the major obstacles to attaining agricultural growth by distributing land to the tillers. Peasant associations were established and recognized as the focal point of development and local organization. This led to the rising expectation that the development potential of the country would be unleashed. In practice, however, the Agrarian Reform did not adequately capture the interest of the peasant sector nor did it mobilize the peasantry to create surplus for re-investment in recently established peasant institutions.

The smallholder peasant sector comprises 90% of the agricultural labor forces and produces 94% of the nation's cereals, pulses and oil seeds. Efforts to stimulate the agricultural sector began in the 1960's, but they were primarily directed toward large-scale mechanized production of export crops. With no institutional mechanism to articulate the plight of peasant farmers, the government's development plan made hardly any investment in peasant agriculture. It was the Third Five Year Development Plan (1968-73) that gave importance to peasant agriculture and introduced the *package program* which involved distributing fertilizer and improved seed to small-scale and subsistence farmers. These innovations were known as the *green revolution* inputs. (6)

The *package program* was first implemented in the Chilalo districts of the Arsi region with the assistance of the Swedish government. Realizing that the *package program* was an appropriate strategy for introducing agricultural innovation to traditional peasant farmers (and for stimulating the agricultural potential of the Arsi region), the Swedish International Development Authority (SIDA) initiated the first integrated rural development project in Arsi. (7) The project known as the Chilalo Agricultural Development Unit (CADU) began in 1967 in Arsi region's Chilalo Awraja.

Ethiopia is divided into 14 administrative regions. Each administrative region is further divided into Awrajas and Weredas. The Arsi region has three Awrajas and 22 Weredas. (See Figure 2)

The CADU program, which lasted from 1967 to 1975, brought an increase in agricultural production and income to participating farmers. But big landowners disproportionately benefited by receiving more of the *green revolution* inputs available through CADU than the small farmers received. (8) Yet, CADU's *package approach* influenced national agricultural policies in Ethiopia during the 1971-75 period. It inspired the nationwide Minimum Package Program (MPP) in effect today. This World Bank funded project provides credit towards the purchase of fertilizer and improved seed to peasant farmers so that they may buy the minimum inputs (fertilizer and improved seed) through extension agents located along all-weather roads in Ethiopia. (9) CADU was renamed the Arsi Rural Development Unit (ARDU) following the 1975 Agrarian Reform. ARDU covers all the three Awrajas (Chilalo, Ticho and Arbagugu) in the Arsi region.

ARDU is still the only integrated rural development program in Ethiopia with the objective of increasing the income and agricultural productivity of peasant farmers. Its emphasis has not truly reflected its objective since March 1975, when the most radical Agrarian Reform programs in Africa unfolded in Ethiopia. The Reform abolished tenancy, service obligation and made land the "collective property of the Ethiopian people." The Reform allowed every household to cultivate up to 10 hectares of land, without ownership, established the peasant association, and empowered them with the right to implement the land reform and promote local self government. The government also gave further directives in 1978 and 1979 for the establishment of service and producer cooperatives that would gradually introduce collective forms of production to the peasant sector. ARDU's programs presently concentrate on the promotion of cooperatives and on the gradual transformation of individual small farms in peasant associations into larger collectively-run farms.

The Ethiopian Revolution and the subsequent agrarian policies dealt decisively with the structural barriers and improved agricultural production. They succeeded in destroying the feudal structure and promoting equity and equality amongst the citizens. The Agrarian Reform has made a genuine attempt to im-

FIGURE 2

Map of Ethiopia and its Regions

Arsi	I	Eritrea	IX	Gamagofa
Asmara	II	Tigrai	X	Bale
	III	Begemdir	XI	Arsi
Addis Ababa	IV	Wollo	XII	Illubabor
	V	Gojjam	XIII	Keffa
	VI	Wollega	XIV	Sidamo
	VII	Shewa		
	VIII	Haraghe		

prove the living standards of peasants through the provisions of education, health, and rural roads, and to narrow the gap between the urban and the rural sectors.

Yet food production has not kept up with population growth; worsening agricultural production is causing both severe food crises in most rural regions and rising food prices for urban dwellers. The average annual agricultural growth between 1974 - 1983 was 1.2 % - considerably lower than the 1965 - 1973 average annual growth rate of 2.1%. In 1985, basic indicators revealed that with a *per capita* income of $120, Ethiopia's status has further deteriorated among those countries classified as having low-income economies. (10) To be sure, the efforts of the Ethiopian Revolution have been partially successful. The rural population has more access to schools, clinics and other social services. Literacy level, for instance, is reported to have risen from 3% to 60% nationally. (11) Peasants have relatively more food to consume (with the exception of the drought-stricken areas) and pay less in land and agricultural taxes.

Moreover, the Agrarian Reform has created important peasant institutions and cooperative societies that could bring a sustainable growth in agriculture. Peasant institutions could mobilize labor to construct schools, clinics, rural roads, provide drinking water and other social services. In Arsi, for example, a number of service cooperatives are actively involved in promoting such activities and in generating surplus which they use for buying agricultural inputs, modern equipment, and flour mills. They are also undertaking reforestation, water and soil conservation, and small irrigation projects that assist in protecting the ecology and preventing future famine.

Given the lack of capital to generate investment in poor countries like Ethiopia, labor and farming equipment such as oxen could be shared under the auspices of the cooperative societies to create investable surplus for the peasant sector. For instance, this study revealed that shortage of oxen is one of the most serious problems facing a considerable number of farmers even in a relatively prosperous region like Arsi. In the famine-stricken areas of the north, lack of draft animals is the single most persistent problem affecting a vast number of farmers. By pooling oxen and other farm implements farmers could plough more land in less time. This could result in the expansion of cultivatable land, which is a major way of increasing agricultural production. Hence, by strategically organizing the existing abundant supply of labor, the cooperative movement presents the potential for improving production as well as social service in rural Ethiopia. As two experienced and informed scholars of the Ethiopian situation expressed it, "it is hard to imagine how anyone could seriously believe a half-starved, impoverished peasant working on his own with almost no capital could be a vehicle for rapid development." (12)

Dramatic improvement in agricultural growth is urgently needed in Ethiopia. But the government's foremost objective in the cooperative movement appears to be to transform family farms into large-scale mechanized farms under the collective form of production. The government considers large-scale collective farms superior to small farms. But the experience of developing countries, however, demonstrates that small farmers who have access to modern inputs have higher levels of productivity and efficiency per unit area than large farms. (13)

Until now, large-scale mechanized agriculture in Ethiopia, under the state farm system has not shown any promise as a source of generating growth. State farms have been consistently in debt and are heavily dependent upon government subsidies in order to operate. Hence, it seems more appropriate for the government to set a short term objective that recognizes the cooperative movement to be a major means of initiating labor-intensive ventures that could create the surplus essential for sustainable growth in the peasant sector. After all, as the findings from this study indicate, collectivization, even in Arsi, which is one of the most politically progressive regions, is at present unpopular among many farmers.

Clearly, the potential to bring a substantial improvement in peasant production was created by the Agrarian Reform. But it has not yet been successful. The government's investment in the peasant sector as compared to the state farm is insignificant in terms of the provision of inputs, credit, appropriate technology, extension services, and infrastructure such as roads, storage and processing facilities. The marketing and the distribution systems dominated by government agencies don't provide adequate incentives for peasant farmers to produce marketed surplus. The prices farmers receive are lower than the open market prices. The supply of consumer goods to the peasant sector is very limited and farmers face serious shortages of household as well as manufactured goods. This also lowers peasant incentive for increased production.

Increased investment in the peasant sector is essential to promote growth in agriculture. It is only by generating growth in peasant agriculture that there could be surplus to be invested in the rural as well as the urban sectors of the economy in Ethiopia. Nevertheless, the present Ten Year Development Plan only allocates 11% of the total investment to the agricultural sector. And most of this is earmarked for organizing peasants in collective forms of production. Hence, the neglect of the smallholder peasant sector and the lack of efficient use of the peasant institutions (that is, the creation of a surplus fund to be invested for future development) are the major obstacles to the attainment of agricultural growth in the peasant sector.

II. The Objective of the Study

Based on a field survey and participant observation, this study examines the perspective of peasant farmers in the Arsi region, focusing on the conditions that constrain their agricultural productivity as well as the potential to increase it. It also presents an empirical analysis of the peasants' perceptions of the emerging peasant and government institutions that are to promote economic and social development as well as to serve as a vehicle to attain agrarian socialism. At present, the government's desire to create these institutions, particularly the promotion of producer cooperatives, is contradicted by the will of the majority of the farmers.

The findings from the Arsi region have considerable national significance. Arsi is one of the few surplus cereal-producing regions in Ethiopia. It has successfully implemented the only integrated rural development programs in Ethiopia, namely CADU and ARDU, under two fundamentally different political environments. These projects have made a significant economic and social impact. Peasant farmers in Arsi are relatively more productive, and politically and socially more aware, and progressive than those in other region in Ethiopia. The Agrarian Reform enjoyed the most popular support in this region. This is largely because nearly half of the farmers before 1975 were tenants in Arsi. Thus, the views and the problems faced by Arsi farmers is likely to have serious implications for the nation's attempt to attain food self-sufficiency and to increase the productivity of the peasant sector.

The study specifically investigates the following research questions:

1. Has the Agrarian Reform altered some of the characteristics of peasant farming?
2. Do peasant farmers consider their cultivatable land to be increasing, decreasing, or remaining the same as before the Agrarian Reform? If there is a change in average cultivated area among farmers, what are the implications of this change for agricultural output in the peasant sector?
3. Did the Agrarian Reform have any effect on land fragmentation? Did peasant farmers find that land fragmentation impeded their productivity?
4. What are the farmers' perceptions of the long-term tenure of their land? What factors influence the farmers' view of land tenure security? Have farmers made investments in their farms since the Agrarian Reform?
5. Is there a considerable difference in the size and membership of a peasant association across regions and ecological zones? What sort of problem is this likely to pose in the long-term? What is the peasant's view of the peasant association? What factors contribute to better administration in the peasant as-

sociation? Is there mismanagement or corruption in the administration of peasant associations?

6. How do farmers view the services provided by the service cooperatives? What reasons are cited for their satisfaction or their dissatisfaction with the service cooperatives? Is there mismanagement or corruption in the administration of service cooperatives?

7. Do peasant farmers understand the government's *stage-by-stage* transformation of peasant associations into producer cooperatives? If farmers had their choice, would they like to remain smallholders or eventually join producer cooperatives as the government intends? What reasons do farmers give for wanting to remain smallholders or join producer cooperatives?

8. What is the nature of the relationship between peasant institutions and government agencies in marketing and distribution and the extension services that are to promote the socialization of the agricultural sector? What are the peasant farmers' perceptions of the present government's marketing and distribution system? What reasons do they cite for liking or disliking the marketing and the distribution system? Has the present marketing arrangement for agricultural products and the distribution system for consumer goods to the peasant sector affected farmers' incentives to increase agricultural production? Is the extension service effective in meeting the needs of both men and women household members ?

9. What is the impact of the Agrarian Reform on peasant farmer production, income, credit participation, farm technology, farming practices and social services?

10. What would be a viable strategy that could reconcile the competition between the smallholder and collective farms to improve the agricultural performance of the peasant sector?

III. The Approach of the Study

The answers to these research questions are based on the analysis of peasant farmers' responses to a survey questionnaire, an *in-depth* interview with peasant association leaders and extension agents, and my own participant observation during the field work.

A questionnaire was designed and pre-tested among farmers from three different ecological zones - highland, medium altitude and lowland - representing the three climatic zones in the Arsi region. Based on the responses obtained during the pre-testing, the questionnaire was revised. The final draft of the questionnaire was used in conducting 150 interviews among randomly selected rural heads of households from 30 peasant associations. Peasant associations were stratified by Awraja and ecological zones to reduce significantly any systematic bias in the sampled population. Five heads of household were randomly selected from each peasant association for an interview. Since Chilalo is the most populous Awraja producing about 60% of the cereal in Arsi, 57% of the sampled population were from Chilalo, 23% from Ticho and 20% from Arbagugu Awraja.

IV. Limitation of the Study

In light of the political, administrative and financial constraints faced in undertaking the field work, a research decision was made not to take a rigorous scientific approach which would involve generating relational hypotheses, testing them, and converting them into empirical generalizations. Instead, this research seeks to develop new sources of data to answer the above research questions as well as to generate new ideas and hypotheses. (14)

This study probes the possibility of statistical relationships among variables, without establishing them, and suggests topics for further social research. These efforts may assist in identifying the obstacles faced by peasant farmers to the improvement of their agricultural production. In addition, through the generation of hypotheses, it may also contribute to work of others who would like to attain higher standards of empirical research.

Gathering data through field interviews (Author).

12

Notes

1. *The New York Times*, New York: May 27, 1986, p.1.

2. *Toward a Sustained Development in Sub-Saharan Africa*, The World Bank, Washington D.C., 1984, p. 20.

3. Ibid, pp. 9-11.

4. These themes are found in : Donald N. Levin, *Wax and Gold: Tradition and Innovation in Ethiopian Culture*, Chicago: University of Chicago Press, 1965.

Richard D. Greenfield, *Ethiopia, a New Political History*, London: Pall Mall Press, 1965.

Robert L Hess, *Ethiopia: The Modernization of Autocracy*, Ithaca, N.Y.: Cornell University Press, 1970.

5. Some of the important studies on land tenure are:

Patrick Gilkes, *The Dying Lion: Feudalism and Modernization in Ethiopia*, London:Julian Friedman, 1975.

Allen Hoben, *Land Tenure Among the Amhare of Ethiopia: The Dynamics of Cognitive Descent*, Chicago: University of Chicago Press, 1973.

Marina and David Ottoway, *Ethiopia: Empire in a Revolution*, New York: African Publishing Company, 1978.

Michael Stahl, *Contradiction in Agricultural Development: A Study of Three Minimum Package Programs in Southern Ethiopia*, Uppsala: Scandinavian Institute of African Studies, Report No. 14, 1973.

John Markakis, *Ethiopia: Anatomy of a Traditional Polity*, Oxford: Clarendon Press, 1974.

6. Seleshi Sisaye and Eileen Stommes, "The Administration of Agricultural Development Programs: A Look at the Ethiopian Approach," *Agricultural Administration*, Vol. 6, No. 3, 1979, pp. 221-226.

7. Benget Nekby, *CADU: An Ethiopian Experiment in Developing Peasant Farming*, Stockholm: Primisa Publishers, 1971, p.47.

8. Henock Kifle, *An Analysis of the CADU Credit Programs 1968/69 - 1970/71 and its Effects on Income Distribution*, Asella: CADU Publication No. 66, 1971. pp. 5-20.

9. Invgar Jonsson, *Diffusion of Agricultural Innovations in Chilalo Awraja*, Addis Ababa: IDR Research Report no. 17., 1975. See also

Extension Project Implementation Department (EPID), *Minimum Package Project Programme Loan Application to IBRID/IIDA*, Addis Ababa, Ministry of Agriculture, EPID Publication No. 6, July 1972.

Solomon Bekure, et al., *Evaluation of the Arsi Rural Development Unit, 1981*. Uppsala, Swedish University of Agricultural Science, September 1981.

10. *World Development Report, 1985*, Washington D.C.: The World Bank, 1985, pp. 174-176.

11. Judith Miller, "The Birth of a New Ethiopia: From Feudalism to Marxism," *The New York Times*, October 8, 1984, p. 1. This figure is likely to be exaggerated by the government for political reasons.

12. Keith Griffin and Roger Hay, "Problems of Agricultural Development in Socialist Ethiopia: An Overview and a Suggested Strategy," *The Journal of Peasant Studies*, Vol. 13, No. 1, October 1985, p.62.

13. Giovanni Andrea Cornia, " Farm Size, Land Yields and the Agricultural production Function : An Analysis of Fitteen Developing Countries," *World Development*, Vol. 13, No. 4, pp. 513-534.

14. Philip Bernard, *Social Research: Strategy and Tactics*, 2nd Edition, New York: The MacMillan Company, 1977.

Chapter 2

The Characteristics of Peasant Farmers

A. The Setting

The Arsi Administrative Region is situated south-west of Ethiopia's capital city, Addis Ababa. It covers 24,000 square kilometers and has a population of 1.7 million. Most of the Arsi region is well suited for agricultural and livestock production. The agricultural system is significantly affected by altitude, which is the most critical indicator of climate in Arsi as well as in Ethiopia. Altitude is also correlated to soil type, vegetation and land use. Based on altitude, three ecological zones are identified in Arsi. (1) These are :

1. Highland (above 2,400 meters);
2. Medium Altitude (between 2000 to 2400 meters)
3. Lowland (below 2000 meters).

The above classification is complicated by the great diversity in ecological zones in areas that are in close proximity to one another, and at times even in the same Peasant Association. In general, large areas of Chilalo are found in highland, Ticho in medium altitude, and Arbagugu in lowland zone.

There are three seasons in most of the highland areas of Ethiopia, including Arsi. These include "the dry season" (*Bega*, November to February), "the big rainy season"(*Keremet*, June to September), and "the small rainy season"(*Belg*,

Oxen used for plowing and threshing: the most important power source for Ethiopian agriculture.

February to May). With the exception of the arid lowland areas in eastern Arbagugu, the rest of Arsi receives adequate rainfall and therefore is well suited for rain feed production of wheat, barley, teff, maize, peas, beans, pulses and oil crops. Arsi is one of the few surplus cereal-producing regions in Ethiopia.

The dominant ethnic group in Arsi is the Oromos. They comprise 81% of the population (60% Arsi Oromos and 21% Shoa Oramos) while 17% are Amharas. About 61% are Muslims and 39% Christians. (2) Nearly all Arsi Oromos are Muslims while all Amhares and most of the Shoa Oromas are Christians. The Arsi Oromos, who were nomads, migrated from the horn of Africa to the highlands of the Arsi region in the sixteen century when a vacuum was created in this region during a conflict between Islamic forces and Christian Amhara groups. Emperor Menlik II conquered the region and brought it under the rule of Imperial Ethiopia in the 1880's. Encouraged by the government's granting of land to new settlers, and the news about the region's fertile soil, the Christian Amharas and Shoa Oromos from the north began to settle in Arsi in large numbers. This process has made most of the Christian Amharas landowners in fertile highland areas and Arsi Oromos tenants on their tribal land, while others moved to settle in the sparsely populated lowland areas.

Peasant farmers comprise 90% of Arsi's population and cultivate an average of two hectares of land. The typical settlement pattern is scattered huts with thatched roofs surrounded by small woods and eucalyptus trees. Most of them live in the relatively fertile medium altitude and highland zones and are engaged in cereal production. Wheat and barley are the two major cash crops. Most of the farmers raise livestock for domestic consumption. But there are a few regions where dairy farming is the main source of income and there are still some pastoralists in the vast lowland areas of Arbagugu.

B. The Integrated Rural Development Project in Arsi

The introduction of Swedish-funded integrated rural development projects has made a profound economic, social and political impact on Arsi farmers. The Chilalo Agricultural Development Unit(CADU) was the first integrated rural development project in Ethiopia. It began in 1967 in Chilalo Awraja. CADU combined the functions of several ministries in one unit, these primarily included adaptive research on crop and livestock production, input supply and dissemination of proven technologies, credit and marketing services, soil and water conservation, forestry, and building of health services. Among its major objectives were balanced economic and social development among small farmers through increased productivity and income, and dissemination of new extension technology for later application in other regions of Ethiopia. (3)

To attain a rapid increase in agricultural production, the first phase of CADU (1967-71) concentrated on providing fertilizer and improved seed to farmers through credit. High-yielding varieties of wheat and barley were the major crops introduced to farmers. Fertilizer consumption by the project participants increased from a total of 42 qts. in full in 1967 to 41,995 in 1971. (4)

During this period, the Swedish technical assistance staff filled most of the positions on the project. CADU's first phase did meet its principal objective of increasing agricultural production: average wheat yield increased from 9.6 qt/ha. to 15.8 qt./ha., and total production increased from 26,000 tons to 74,000 tons over the same period. (5)

CADU's second phase (1971-75) saw fertilizer consumption soar to a total of 70,604 qts. as well as a dramatic increase in the use of credit and high-yielding varieties. (6) CADU diversified its activities toward improvement in cultural practices and other crops such as barley. Crop yields of participating farmers increased 70 to 100 percent and milk production from cross-bred heifers was 10 times greater than from local cows. (7)

Prior to 1975, about 50% of the farmers in Arsi were tenants. The application of high-yielding varieties and fertilizer made mechanized farming very profitable. Witnessing the profit, landlords and even rich merchant elites invested heavily in land. This resulted in widespread tenant eviction and excessive land rents. (8) Owners of over 10 hectares of land constituted the largest number of credit participants. Yet, tenants were supposed to be the principal beneficiaries. (9) Consequently, in the second phase, CADU tried to counteract this trend by excluding large farmers who owned over 10 hectares from its credit program and denying credit to landowners who did not sign temporary leases for their tenants.

The Third Phase (1976 to 1986) operates in a different environment; during the past ten years peasant associations have been created and the 1975 Agrarian Reform has been implemented. CADU expanded its program to Ticho and Arbagugu Awraja. It was renamed the Arsi Rural Development Unit, and covered the entire Arsi region. Although ARDU still employed the "*package approach*" of CADU (ie. input distribution and extension) to increase peasant farmers' production, it also emphasized the establishment of cooperative societies to bring about a socialist transformation of the peasant sector.

Peasant farmer displaying the traditional farm implements (above).
Peasant in front of forestry project (below).

C. Important Crops and Animals

The major crops grown in Arsi are wheat, barley, maize, sorghum, teff, beans and peas. Crop farming is the single most important source of cash earnings for Arsi farmers - particularly wheat and barley. Since the establishment of CADU, emphasis has been placed upon producing improved varieties of wheat and barley. The 1980 ARDU survey underscored the importance of wheat and barley to peasant agriculture by indicating that 71% of the cultivated area in Chilalo, 55% in Ticho, and 31% in Arbagugu was given over to wheat and barley. (10)

CADU/ARDU has been particularly successful in disseminating improved varieties of wheat. The findings from this survey also confirm that wheat followed by barley were considered to be the most important crops by the majority of the sampled farmers. In addition, a significant statistical relationship was found between the primary crops farmers grow in the Awraja, and the type of ecological zone in which they live. In both Chilalo and Ticho Awraja, wheat was considered to be the primary crop by the majority of farmers. The ecological zones of most of Chilalo and Ticho are suited for wheat cultivation. Most of the respondents in Arbagugu indicated that sorghum and maize were their most important crops. Both crops are also well adapted to most of the lowland areas in Arbagugu. All the farmers who indicated maize as their primary crop in Chilalo live in the Dhera area, which is the lowland zone. The highland zone is well adapted to wheat and barley, medium altitude to wheat and teff, lowland to sorghum and maize.

At present, ARDU's four crop experiment stations and seed multiplication farms are concentrated in the highlands of Chilalo Awraja and are mainly concerned with wheat and barley crops. This has limited improved seed availability to farmers living in Arbagugu and Ticho Awraja.

Peasant farmers generally keep a pair of oxen to plow, cows for milk, and a few sheep and goat for consumption. Oxen, which are used for ploughing and treshing, are the single most important animals to the overwhelming number of farmers. The only exception, a case in which cows were considered more important than oxen, was in livestock areas like Koffele (Chilalo Awraja) where the farmers derive a substantial portion of their income from the sale of milk and milk products.

D. Cultivatable Land and Types of Production

All cultivatable land in Ethiopia is managed under three types of production systems. These include smallholder (peasant) farms, producer cooperatives and

State Farms. The production systems that would be suitable to Ethiopian agriculture will be discussed in Chapter 7.

The smallholder or peasant farming sector, is the dominant sector in Ethiopia's economy. Smallholder peasants are organized into peasant associations. They constitute about 90% of the agricultural labor force and cultivate 94% of the crop land. Smallholders in a peasant association are encouraged to pool their land and implements to form producer cooperatives. Members of a producer cooperative cultivate their land collectively and share the produce based on labor contribution. The government's long-term objective is to transform smallholders into collective farmers by inducing them to join producer cooperatives. Hence, within peasant associations there exist both the smallholder and the producer cooperative sectors. However, peasant farmers in producer cooperatives only make up 3% of the rural households, and farm 2% of the cultivated land.

In Arsi, where vigorous efforts have been launched by extension agents to attract peasants to join producer cooperatives, 7% of the rural farm families are members of producer cooperatives, and cultivate 11% of the land. Preliminary studies at the national level in general, and in Arsi in particular, indicate that the average size of land per farm family is slightly larger among peasants organized in producer cooperatives than those farming as smallholders in peasant associations. (11)

The State Farms were created after the Agrarian Reform to manage the 5000 commercial farms which have a total area of 67,250 hectares. The mechanized commercial farms were not suitable to be distributed to peasant farmers and most of them were converted into State Farms. In 1979, the Ministry of State Farming was established: the revolutionary government wanted to secure a reliable flow of food to urban dwellers, the military and other government institutions during the period of uncertainty accompanying the impact of the Agrarian Reform on peasant production. The State Farm sector rapidly expanded to over 245,000 hectares by 1982, using 4% of the nation's cultivated land. Wheat, maize and sorghum make up 60% of the crop land, and the rest of the land is used for export crops such as coffee, cotton and pulses. The State Farm is still a small sector employing 4% of the labor force and contributing 5% of the agricultural output. Yet it receives three-fourths of the nation's resources in terms of credit, fertilizer and improved seeds. (12)

In the absence of improved farming technology, expanding cultivatable land is a realistic means of increasing agricultural production in Africa. In fact, 80% of the increase in agricultural output in Africa has been attained through the expansion of cultivated land. (13) Land is relatively abundant in Ethiopia and a significant amount of it could be expanded through labor mobilization. It is estimated that out of the 75 to 85 million hectares of agricultural land in Ethiopia, only 12 to 13 million hectares (16%) are used for crops and fallow. (14) For instance, a recent study indicated that in the west and south of the central high-lands alone, 30% of the arable land remains fallow. Reducing the fallow areas by 50% would increase the crop land by about 8% in Ethiopia. (15) Conse-quently, the government should be seriously concerned with the development of ways in which to expand cultivatable land; these ways will be discussed in detail in Chapter 7.

In Arsi, the cultivated area under the management of smallholders has markedly increased by both the government's and ARDU's accounts. Intensive cultivation spread from Chilalo (where CADU operated) to other Awrajas in the Arsi region in the late 1970s. The increase in population, and the availability of improved agricultural inputs through the integrated rural development project, has made it possible for vast amounts of forest to be cleared for crop cultivation. Cultivated area is reported to have increased from about 400,000 hectares in 1974 to 500,000 hectares in 1984. (16) ARDU has played a major role in the expansion of cultivatable land. Its extension agents work with the government administrators to bring idle land under state or peasant association control.

In spite of the significant increase in cultivatable land in Arsi, there is no cor-responding increase in the average amount of cultivatable land per farm family. The comparison of several surveys presented in Table 1 proves this fact.

Table 1

Comparison of Surveys Indicating Average Cultivated Area in Arsi

Type of Survey	Cultivated Area/Household
1974 National Sample Survey	2.9 ha.
1980 ARDU Survey	2.2 ha.
1984 Agricultural Sample Survey	2.1 ha.
1984 Dejene Survey	2.0 ha.

The findings in Table 1 show that the average area of cultivatable land has decreased from about 3 ha. before 1974 to 2 ha. in 1984. What may be the pos-sible reasons for this decrease?

1. The 1975 Rural Land Proclamation entitles anyone over 18 years old to have his or her own plot as a member of a peasant association. There has also been a rapid rural population growth rate in Arsi. It is conceivable that

these factors may have substantially increased the number of rural house-holds that are sharing this expanded land.

2. Since the initial 1975 distribution of land, nearly 50% of the sampled farmers have indicated that second stage adjustment of the land has occurred in their peasant association and 65% of these farmers indicated a decrease in cultivated area after redistribution. This suggests that more people are join-ing peasant associations as new members without an expansion in the size of peasant associations. Thus, change in the composition of peasant associa-tions is likely to have an adverse effect on the size of cultivated area per rural household.

3. Most of the expanded land may have been given to State Farms or pro-ducer cooperatives or used in government resettlement schemes.

There is no reliable data to assess whether land under peasant cultivation has increased in absolute figures in other regions of Ethiopia following the Agrarian Reform. But it is clear that the Reform has made little impact on the size of cultivatable land per rural household in other regions of Ethiopia; as Table 2 in-dicates, the average holding of a rural household in most regions is under 2 hectares. (17)

Table 2

Average size of Per Capita Holding by Region

Administrative Region	Hectares per Holding
Arsi	2.16
Bale	1.18
Gomogofa	0.86
Gojam	1.80
Gondar	1.90
Hararghe	0.91
Illubabor	1.09
Kaffa	0.86
Shoa	1.39
Sidamo	0.58
Wollega	1.59
Wollo	1.57

The Rural Land Proclamation stated that farm families could cultivate up to 10 hectares of land. This inevitably aroused the expectations of the land-hungry peasants. But, in reality, the great majority of peasant farmers still cultivate relatively the same size of land as before. This is because the Proclamation gave tenants and landless laborers the rights to the land they cultivate without private ownership. In addition to the government surveys, two recent independent studies confirm that Ethiopian agriculture is still dominated by peasants operating small plots. The first study covered 20 highland peasant associations in 10 administrative regions (which included Arsi) and found that the average cultivatable land per farm family is 1.5 hectares. (18) The second survey was based on four different regions - southern, south-western, western and northern regions of Ethiopia. The study indicated that 60% of the sampled farmers presently cultivate less than 1 hectare and 40% between 1 to 2 hectares, whereas these figures were 56% and 25% respectively prior to the Agrarian Reform. (19)

The findings from Arsi as well as from other regions of Ethiopia suggest that landholding per capita of peasant farmers is likely to decrease under the present conditions. Peasant associations cannot continue to redistribute land to new members without a corresponding expansion in the size of the association. Mini-plots of under 1 hectare are not well suited to the application of improved agricultural inputs. Hence, diminutive landholding per capita poses serious constraints to improvement in agricultural output as well as to the ecology of the area.

The government assumes that 10 ha. is an ideal size for a farm family. Other studies have also suggested that farmers can operate 10 hectares effectively. (20) Field experience indicates this assumption is impractical. Without an improvement in farming technology, even farmers in Arsi, who have more access to extension services and inputs than other regions in Ethiopia could not effectively operate more than 5 hectares. The findings from Arsi support Dessalegn Rahmato's argument that about 5 hectares would be the appropriate size for most peasant families to operate efficiently at the moment. (21)

The sampled farmers in Arsi were asked if their cultivatable area has increased, decreased, or remained the same since the 1975 Agrarian Reform. Slightly more farmers, 44% responded that their cultivatable land had increased, 41% that it had decreased, and 15% that no change had occurred. Again, given the large increase in total land expansion in Arsi, the percentage of respondents with an increase in cultivatable land is insignificant.

In an attempt to understand the special characteristics of farmers who reported an increase or decrease in cultivated area, these findings were cross-tabulated by Awraja, ecological zone, status of farmers before the Agrarian Reform, land redistribution in peasant association since 1976, change in land size after redistribution in the peasant association, change in agricultural production, and change in the number of households in a peasant association. A statistically significant relationship was found between change in cultivated area and change in land size after the initial redistribution, and between change in agricultural production and income.

Although there was no statistical relationship between size of cultivated area and status of farmer, further analysis revealed that 65% of the former tenants indicated an increase in their cultivated area after 1975 as opposed to 27% of the former owner-cultivators. A 50-year-old farmer tenant with 8 children in Chilalo Awraja is an example of a former tenant who now reports a decrease in cultivated area. In the initial 1975 land distribution he received the same plot of land of 2.5 ha. he cultivated before the Reform. Then another land redistribution occurred in his peasant association in 1978, as new members joined. As the result of this land adjustment, his holdings have decreased to 2 hectares.

Whether a peasant association has undertaken land adjustment since the initial redistribution is an important factor influencing the size of the present landholding. Most of the respondents, 88%, whose cultivated area has decreased indicated that land adjustment has occurred in their peasant association, resulting in a decrease in their cultivatable land. The observed statistical relationship between change in cultivated area and agricultural production as well as income will be examined in the section on agricultural production in Chapter 6.

E. Land Fragmentation

Another characteristic of peasant farming in Ethiopia is the pattern of fragmented holdings scattered in several places close by and further away from the homestead. The literature argues that the previous land tenure system may have resulted in more fragmented holdings because of the inheritance law and population pressure. The Agrarian Reform has effectively abolished the inheritance system that entitled each heir to an equal portion of land. It also attempts to bring about land consolidation through a second stage distribution of land within peasant associations.

It is difficult to assess the impact of the Agrarian Reform on land fragmentation, since detailed data on this issue both before and after the Agrarian Reform is required. Nevertheless, the comparison of this survey with that of the government taken prior to the Reform provides useful insights into the issue of fragmentation. In this survey 75% of the respondents have two or more parcels in their holdings, whereas the 1966 Central Statistics Office Survey (the only information in this regard in Arsi before the Reform) indicates this number to be 74%. Hence, fragmented holdings are still as widespread in Arsi as they were prior to the Agrarian Reform.

The literature on land fragmentation generally agrees that it: (a) discourages soil conservation practices, (b) makes "impractical" use of fertilizer and other inputs, (C) reduces the profitability of agricultural investment, (d) reduces agricultural productivity and income of individual farmers, (e) reduces risk-taking and agricultural innovation and (f) weakens the rural economy. (22)

During the field survey, the adverse effects of land fragmentation on peasant production were observed when farmers had more than three parcels per holding and each parcel was smaller than a half hectare and further away from the homestead. On the other hand, the benefits of fragmented holdings were observed in some peasant associations which exhibited highland and medium altitude or medium altitude and lowland agro-climatic conditions. In Seru RDC (Ticho Awraja), a 55-year-old farmer pointed out that most farmers had always had at least two parcels in the surrounding areas for as long as he could remember. His peasant association has a hilly area which is classified as a medium altitude and an extensive lowland area within a few miles of the hill. This farmer grows teff in his parcel in the hilly area and uses his holdings in the lowlands to grow sorghum and to feed livestock. His situation supports Michael Collinson's argument that land fragmentation "*spreads risks*" associated with micro-climatic variations, pests, and diseases. (23)

In cases where the peasant association has tried to promote equity in the quality of land to its members, the Agrarian Reform may have contributed to more fragmented holdings. For instance, some peasant associations in Chilalo have developed different categories of land based on soil fertility and topography. In their attempt to promote equity, peasant association leaders distribute land from all categories. As a result, a farmer's holding is scattered in various areas of the peasant association. This is particularly true in some of the highland peasant associations where flooding and erosion are more of a problem in some areas than in others in the same peasant association. A recent study also indicates that peasant associations which emphasized equity in land quality have increased the incidence of land parcelization. (24)

Peasant association leaders and peasants seem to be more concerned with promoting equity in size and quality of land rather than with land consolidation. This seems to contradict the government's belief that more consolidation will take place within the peasant association through further redistribution.

The findings from this study show that the majority of the sampled farmers (75%) presently have at least two of the same parcels in their holdings as they had before the Agrarian Reform. Consequently, it is difficult to draw conclusions on the effect of the Agrarian Reform on land fragmentation. It was beyond the scope of the study to generate and analyze data on this issue. But it is an important issue for future study and specific questions should be asked on the number of parcels per holding, their size, their distance from the homestead and their level of fertility. This will enable us to better understand the impact of the

Agrarian Reform on land fragmentation as well as its adverse and beneficial effects on production.

Notes

1. Betru Haile, *On the Activities of the Plant Husbandry Department*, ARDU Publication No. 24, Asella, 1983.

2. *Central Statistic Office*, Statistical Bulletin 46, Addis Ababa: Ethiopia, 1985.

3. Seleshi Sisaye,"Swedish Development Aid Policy: A Discussion with Reference to Ethiopia", *Public Administration and Development*, Vol. 2, 1982, pp. 147-167. See also

Benget Nekby, *CADU: An Ethiopian Experiment in Developing Peasant Farming*, Stockholm: Prisma Publisher, 1971.

4. *ARDU: Objectives, Activities, Inputs, Prospects and Problems*, Asella, 1984, p. 10. See also:

Tesfai Tecle, "An Approach to Rural Development: A Case Study of the Ethiopian Package Projects," *Rural Africana, No. 28.*, East Lansing: Michigan, Michigan State University, 1975, pp. 87-105.

5. Guy Hunter et al, *Final Report of the Appraisal of CADU and EPID*, Stockholm: Sweden, 1974, p.6.

6. *ARDU: Objectives, Activities, Inputs, Prospects and Problems*, Asella: Ethiopia, 1984, p.10.

Solomon Bekure, et al, *Evaluation of the Arsi Rural Development Unit, 1981*, Uppsala: Sweden, Swedish University of Agricultural Science, September 1981.

7. Betru Gebregziabher, *Integrated Development in Rural Ethiopia: An Evaluation Study of the Chilalo Agricultural Development Unit*, Bloomington: Indiana, Pastiam, 1975.

8. Tesfai Tecle, *The Evolution of Alternative Rural Development Strategies in Ethiopia: The Implication for Employment and Income Distribution*, East Lansing: Michigan, African Rural Employment Paper No. 12, Michigan State University, 1975.

9. Henock Kifle, *An Analysis of the CADU Credit Programs 1968/69 - 1970/71 and its Effects on Income Distribution*, Asella, CADU Publication No. 66, 1971, pp. 5-20.

10. *Investigation on the Impact of the Agrarian Reform on Peasants' Income and Expenditure Patterns*, Asella: Ethiopia, Planning, Evaluation and Budget Section, ARDU Publication No. 18, October 1981, p. 25.

11. *Proposal for SIDA Support to Rural Development in Arsi and Bale 1986/87 - 1988/89*, Stockholm: Sweden, December 1985, pp. 233-234.

12. *Ethiopia: The Agriculture Sector - An Interim Report*, The World Bank, 1983, pp. 19-20.

13. *The Development of Effectiveness of Food Aid in Africa*, New York: New York, Agricultural Development Council, 1982, p. 52.

14. *Ethiopia: Review of Farmers' Incentives and Agricultural Marketing and Distribution Efficiency*, The World Bank, . 1983, pp.19-20.

15. Keith Griffin and Roger Hays, "Problems of Agricultural Development in Socialist Ethiopia: An Overview and a Suggested Strategy," *Journal of Peasant Studies*, Vol. 13, No. 1, October 1985, pp. 53-55.

16. *Proposal for SIDA Support to Rural Development in Arsi and Bale 1986/87 - 1988/89*, Stockholm: Sweden, December 1985, pp. 224-225.

17. The Agricultural Survey, Ministry of Agriculture, Planning and Programing Department, Addis Ababa: Oct. 1984, p. 36.

18. Yeraswork Admassie, Mulugetta Abebe and Markos Ezra, *Ethiopian Highlands Reclamation Study: Report on the Sociological Survey and Sociological Considerations in Preparing a Development Strategy*, Addis Ababa: Ministry of Agriculture, Land Use Planning and Regulatory Department, December 1983.

19. Dessalegn Rahmato, *Agrarian Reform in Ethiopia*. Uppsala: Scandinavian Institute of African Studies, 1984, pp. 52-55.

20. *CADU: Investigation on Mechanized Farming and its Effects on Peasant Agriculture*, Asella: Ethiopia, CADU Report No. 74, 1972, p.79. See also:
Michael Stahl, *Contradiction in Agricultural Development: A Study of Three Minimum Package Programs in Southern Ethiopia*, Uppsala: Scandinavian Institute of African Studies, Report No. 14, 1973.

21. Dessalegn Rahmato, *Agrarian Reform in Ethiopia*. Uppsala: Scandinavian Institute of African Studies, 1984, p. 28.

22. Malcom F Mcpherson, *Land Fragmentation: Adverse? Beneficial? and for Whom?* Cambridge: MA, Development Discussion Paper No. 145, Harvard Institute for International Development, 1983.

23. M.P. Collinson, *Farm Management In Peasant Agriculture*, New York: Prager Publishers, 1972; See also
R.C. Porter, "Risks, Incentives and Techniques of Low-Income Farmers," *The Indian Economic Journal*, Vol. VII, No. 1, 1959, pp. 1-27.

24. Dessalegn Rahmato, *Agrarian Reform in Ethiopia*. Uppsala: Sweden, Scandinavian Institute of African Studies, 1984, pp. 52-56.

Chapter 3

Land Tenure: Implications for Increasing Peasant Production

Land ownership is inextricably linked to political power and social status in agriculturally based economies: the structure of land tenure manifests the political and economic power and class relationships in a society. Nowhere is this as clearly evident as in Ethiopia before the 1975 Agrarian Reform.

Land tenure also plays a major role in determining the ways in which land, labour and other inputs are used to attain higher agricultural output. The government's effort to attain equity in land distribution in itself creates an incentive for increased productivity. Empirical findings from several farm management studies conducted in developing countries have indicated higher yields and greater labor absorption in small farms than in large farms: these findings have greatly strengthened the case for land reform. (1) Needless to say, many scholars have viewed land reform as a key factor in political and economic development. (2)

The definition and outcome of land reform varies from one country to another. Narrowly defined, land reform is the distribution of land to small farmers, tenants and landless laborers. Broadly defined, it encompasses land distribution as well as development programs aimed at increasing agricultural production. (3) In this study the term Agrarian Reform is used to refer to the broad definition of land reform which comprises both equity and productivity. In addition, Agrarian Reform includes the political and economic measures taken to transform the technological and the institutional bases of the society.

Agrarian Reform goes beyond land distribution and the technocratic solution to increase agricultural production through the application of improved inputs. In the Ethiopian case, emphasis was placed on what Ajit Kuma Ghose calls demand (distributional) crisis and not on supply (production) crisis when the government approached the issues of declining food production and rural poverty.

(4) In Ethiopia the distributional and production crises were attributed to the political and the institutional structure; therefore new institutions were created to carry out the Agrarian Reform. As Ghose points out, the solutions to these crises "can only be predicated upon the conscious restructuring of the social relationship of production in agriculture." (5)

The land tenure system in pre-revolutionary Ethiopia was among the most complex in the world and was closely linked with the existing political structure. The debate over whether or not the land tenure system in Ethiopia was a *feudal* one continues. (6) One of the most detailed studies which maintains that the Ethiopian land tenure system was feudal is by Joanna Mantel-Niecko. (7) Mantel-Niecko asserts that Ethiopia was a feudal society based on the subordination of the people to the authorities under three types of serfdom. These were (A) land serfdom, where land use was conditional on the decision of higher authorities; (B) personal serfdom, in terms of bondage to the land or obligation to do services; and (C) legal serfdom, where no legal challenge to the decisions of the overlord was possible. (8)

Despite the continuing debate on the nature and the type of feudalism in pre-revolutionary Ethiopia, most agree that it is possible to identify two land tenure arrangements that existed between and within the different regions of the country. The most important types of tenure were the kinship and the communal land-based tenure of the north, and the private land-based tenure of the south. The north was characterized by small fragmented communal holdings distributed on the basis of hereditary rights. In the south, landlords dominated land in large amounts and tenants cultivated it in small units through various forms of share-cropping and rent arrangements.

The net effect of these land tenure systems in pre-revolutionary Ethiopia was suboptimal fragmented holdings and land degradation in the north, and tenancy, land insecurity, and landlord domination in the south. The exploitative production relationship between a small number of the nobility and landowners and the peasantry was a key structural problem retarding agricultural growth and innovation and increasing rural poverty. (9)

In Arsi, the land tenure system was characterized by a *feudal* pattern in which landlords owned a large amount of land that was farmed by tenants who shared either 1/2 or 1/3 of their total harvest with the landlord. Nearly 50% of the population in Arsi were tenants. (10) Another feature of the land tenure system was land insecurity of tenants who had no legal protection from arbitrary eviction. Tenant eviction and landlessness were especially widespread in Chilalo in the late 1960s and early 1970s as the result of mechanization and the arrival of CADU in 1967. CADU's credit program for the application of improved agricultural inputs favored big land owners instead of peasant farmers as was intended. (11)

The percentage of former tenants and former owner-cultivators before the Agrarian Reform is presented in Table 3.

Table 3

Comparison of Surveys of Former Tenants Before the Agrarian Reform

| Type of Survey | Percentage of Tenancy Among Sampled Households | | | |
	Chilalo	Ticho	Arbagugu	Arsi
1967 Ministry of Land Reform	44	48	58	48
1968 CADU Agricultural Survey	52			
1970 CADU Agricultural Survey	34			
1972 CADU Agricultural Survey	26			
1971 Arussi Provincial Governor's Office	63			
1980 ARDU Survey	71.36	67.37	62.33	67.02
1984 Dejene Survey	62	57	60	61

In this study 61% of the sampled farmers in Arsi were former tenants, and 30% former owner-cultivators. In the 1980 ARDU survey, 67% of the sampled farmers indicated that they had formerly been tenants. But, as indicated in Table 3, most studies have indicated that tenancy in Arsi did not exceed 50%. The reasons for the high discrepancy between the surveys taken before the Agrarian Reform and those taken after the Agrarian Reform are puzzling. It may be partly due to a sampling bias, since a large number of the respondents in both the 1980 and 1984 surveys were from areas where tenancy was widespread. Another explanation is that some farmers may like to identify themselves as former tenants, thinking that it would be advantageous to be viewed as a "repressed" peasant prior to the land reform.

Among the former tenants about one-third of them were evicted from their land prior to the land reform. The majority of them (21%) have regained the same land they cultivated previously. Most of the evicted tenants lived in northern Chilalo. With the coming of CADU, rich landowners and provincial elites introduced tractors in northern Chilalo where the fertile flat land is suitable for large-scale mechanized farming. This has resulted in widespread tenant eviction. The 1971 CADU survey also indicated widespread tenant eviction since tenancy in northern Chilalo, where mechanization is actively taking place, was 13% while in southern Chilalo, where mechanization has not yet begun, tenancy was 54%. (12)

In his 1978 analysis of land reform, "The Death of Land Reform: A Polemic," David Lehman presents two broad theoretical frameworks: a technocratic and a historic one. The first is a reformist and the second is a revolutionary approach to land reform. The technocratic framework employs administrative measures to promote equity and social justice within the existing structures. The historicists, on the other hand, assume that inequality is created and preserved by the productive relationship in a society. Hence, political action is necessary to transform the existing power and institutional structures. (13) Both reformists and revolutionaries believe, as was the case in Ethiopia, that feudalism inhibits agricultural growth and innovation, under-utilizes land and allocates resources inefficiently. But they differ on the ultimate objective of the reform.

The March 1975 Rural Land Proclamation in Ethiopia, a revolutionary one, overthrew the basic political and social structure that had created an enormous inequality in wealth and power along class and ethnic lines. Proclamation No. 31, entitled "A Proclamation to Provide for the Public Ownership of Rural Lands," nationalized all rural lands and limited landholding to ten hectares per rural family. Peasant associations were organized to implement land reform, collect taxes, and assume the functions of local government. Tenants and landless laborers were automatically granted the use of the land they tilled but without private ownership. Land could not be sold, mortgaged or leased. The land reform in Ethiopia was what John K. Galbraith has called "a revolutionary step; it passes power, property and status from one group in the community to another." (14)

The Agrarian Reform in Ethiopia does not seem to fit any of the three typologies developed by Alain de Janvry based on his study of sixty years of land reform in Latin America. Using the concepts of mode of production and social class, de Janvry classified reforms that (A) redistribute land to peasants within the capitalist or pre-capitalist structure; (B) induce transition from pre-capitalist to capitalist agriculture by transforming it into a large-scale capitalist enterprise (junker); and (C) induce a shift from large-scale enterprise to smallholder farming by putting limits on the size of landholding within the capitalist structure. (15) These reforms are redistributive and do not affect the mode of production or class relations. On the other hand, the Agrarian Reform in Ethiopia has profoundly changed the social relationships of the whole society and de Janvry's classification could not explain the Ethiopian experience. Hence, a fourth category, reforms that distribute land to peasants in the context of the gradual trans-formation of peasant farming into socialist agriculture, will make a useful addi-tion to de Janvry's typological system.

Accordingly, given the socialist nature of the Agrarian Reform in Ethiopia, the economic and the political effects of land reform observed by de Janvry in Latin America also do not adequately describe the Ethiopian situation. The con-sequences of land reform found in Latin America were : (A) expansion of do-mestic markets to create an articulated economy through the increased con-sumption and expenditure of peasants; (B) development of capitalism in the non-reform (the modern urban) sector using the reform sector; (C) creation of political stability in the reform sector by giving land to peasants; and (D) main-tenance of functional dualism between the reform (rural) and the non-reform (urban) sector. (16)

The Agrarian Reform was, for the most part, successfully implemented with only minor localized resistance. Peasants in the tenancy-ridden south were more enthusiastic about the Reform than those with a communal tenure in the north. In fact, the government tried to assuage the feelings of the conservative small-holder peasants of the north with Article 19, an amendment that grants peasants possessory right over the land they till. Since tenants in the north are landown-ers themselves, officials of the military government also assured them that the Reform would not confiscate their land or undertake major land redistribution in their region. (17) As a result, the pace of land distribution and peasant associa-tion formation was swift in the south and slow in the north. As Marina Ottoway pointed out, in "Land Reform in Ethiopia," the stronger the antagonism between landlords and peasants, the more promptly the peasants organized into associa-tions, redistributed lands and experimented in collective farming. (18) Ot-toway's assessment has been supported by discussions held during the field work with ARDU extension agents who were involved in the implementation of the reform.

The military regime in power (known as the Derg) did not have the adminis-trative capacity nor the manpower to implement such a radical land reform. Hence, it turned to the university and high school students who were previously of the movement agitating for reform (their national known slogan was "land to the tiller.") These students were soon sent to the countryside through a program known as the "Development Through Cooperation Campaign."

The activities of the student campaign at times coincided with and at other times were in contra-distinction to the military government's objectives; the students had their own hidden agenda. They wanted to radicalize the peasantry while taking an authoritarian attitude towards them. They pushed for the estab-lishment of communal farms for the land-hungry peasants in the south and hoped to mobilize the countryside against the military regime which they con-sidered illegitimate. There was a strong Maoist influence in the student leadership: inexperienced and overzealous, the students wanted as quickly as possible to transform Ethiopia into a communist state, modeled on China, and failed in this attempt. (19)

The following shifting alliances emerged during the implementation of the Agrarian Reform: in the first phase of the implementation of the Reform, the students and the peasants joined forces to combat the landlords. The government supported the students' efforts to teach peasants about the land reform, to neutralize the landlords, establish peasant associations, and push for the involvement of the poorest segment in the leadership of peasant association. But the government became increasingly uneasy when the students incited the peasantry to armed struggle against their class enemy, creating violence and instability in the countryside. An example of such an incident took place outside the town of Jimma (the capital of one of the western provinces) where radical students and their peasant followers imprisoned landowners and some of the police force whom they felt were "anti-revolutionary." The arrest spread in Jimma itself, where several students were reportedly killed. The military intervened to put down the unrest. (20) In the southern region of the Sidamo province similar incidents requiring military intervention occurred, namely in Wollamo Soddo, Dilla and Yirgalem. Student unrest also threatened the flow of food supply to the urban areas during a time when the new regime was facing various threats to its rule. (21)

The second phase began when the government intervened to control the process of the land reform because of the above disruption caused by the student-led rebellion. Also strife between students and peasants developed during this phase. In general, peasants were receptive to the student's enthusiasm for the Reform. But they were reluctant and at times strongly opposed to forming collective farms. In the north, open hostility towards the students was manifested. Even in the south, there was a backlash against the students' attempt to control peasant associations and to inculcate them with revolutionary ideas. In some regions the backlash led to violence that required the military intervention of the government. At this point, the peasants and the government joined forces against the students. And this marked the third phase in the implementation of the Reform.

By the summer of 1976, a little over a year after the student campaign began, most students had realized the failure of their objectives to radicalize and gain the support of the peasantry for their own political ends. They started coming back to the city and the program was soon suspended.

The Student Development through Cooperation Campaign was instrumental to the consolidation of the land reform and to effectively mobilizing the peasantry to combat those who could have undermined the implementation of the Reform. The students also played a key role in the swift formation of the peasant associations. Within just over a year of its operation (April 1975 to June

1976) the student campaign helped to organize 20,000 peasant associations with 5 million households (which accounts for 80% of the peasant associations formed in 1985). At present, there are about 23,500 peasant associations with a total of 7.2 million members. (22)

During the initial stage, the government had left the process of land distribution, peasant association formation and the establishment of cooperative farms in the hands of the peasants. This was mainly due to the government's ideological commitment to making the peasant association an autonomous local government unit and not to the government's limited capacity to control the process, as is frequently argued. This commitment is made evident in Proclamation No. 71, which empowers peasant associations by granting them legal rights to engage in transactions such as acquiring loans for development purposes, promoting cooperatives and self-help activities, setting up judiciary and defense squads to adjudicate disputes and to combat those challenging their authority, and by integrating them into the regional administration through the establishment of the Revolutionary Administrative and Development Committees at the sub-district (Wereda) level.

It was feared that such massive land redistributions and the instability associated with such radical reform would lead to a decrease in peasant production. On the contrary, agricultural output rose by 22.8% after the first year of the Reform. (23) This was largely because the motivation of peasants increased when they became owners of their land and did not have to share their produce. There was also an adequate level of rainfall during that year. The startling growth rate immediately after the Reform did not continue in subsequent years. In fact, since 1980 there has been a sharp decline in peasant production in many regions. Some of the reasons for this decline include civil war, drought, land tenure insecurity, an inefficient marketing and distribution system, and the lack of the generation and the dissemination of agricultural innovations.

As a result of his analysis of the political processes of land reform in *Land Reform and Politics: A Comparative Analysis*, Hung-Chao Tai proposed the following hypotheses: (1) the need for legitimacy prompts the elites to initiate land reform (2) the relationship between the elites and the landed class dictates the formulation and the content of the land reform program and, (3) political commitment affects program implementation. (24) The first two hypotheses seem irrelevant to provide an explanation of the Ethiopian situation. It was the Ethiopian Revolution that subsequently led to the Agrarian Reform. This was mainly due to the ideological commitment of the military rulers and their civilian advisors and the student agitation for reform; the Agrarian Reform in Ethiopia was not initiated to ensure political legitimacy. But its implementation gave the military regime badly needed popular support in the countryside at a time of serious opposition in the urban areas.

Contrary to Tai's second hypothesis, the military regime in Ethiopia did not attempt to resolve its difference with the landed class by minimizing their losses. It went so far as to align itself with the peasantry and to protect their interests. But the third hypothesis, that the degree of political commitment is central to the effective implementation of reform programs, is supported by the Ethiopian experience. At the time of the Rural Land Proclamation, the military regime did not have great administrative capacity: it faced political instability, landlord resistance and a peasantry possessing a minimal political consciousness. In spite of these obstacles, the regime succeeded in implementing the reform in a remarkably short period of time because of its political commitment to reform at all costs.

In order to study the impact of land reform on political structures, Tai identified political participation, national integration, rural institutionalization, stability, and communism as significant features influencing the rate and the direction of transformation. (25) It is helpful to examine his categories to see whether they apply to the Ethiopian condition.

The Agrarian Reform in Ethiopia has mobilized the peasantry towards greater political participation to protect its own interests as well as to provide support for the government. Having introduced peasant institutions for the increased participation of peasants in the political and development activities of their community, the government is ambivalent about allowing these institutions to enjoy greater autonomy. The creation of peasant institutions during the Agrarian Reform (peasant associations, service cooperatives and producer cooperatives) resulted in greater economic and political integration of the regions of Ethiopia. Each peasant association has an elected representative at the district, regional and the national level (the All Ethiopian Peasant Association); the government marketing and distribution agencies can reach the countryside more effectively through these peasant institutions. Such integration may help to extend services and link the peripheral areas to the economic activities at the center. Some have argued that integration has also meant the control of the rural population indirectly through the peasant association and directly through settlement schemes. (26)

Both communists and non-communists have supported the Agrarian Reform in Ethiopia for different reasons. Though by far the minority, communist-inspired movements have greatly influenced the military government policy towards the land reform. Other socialist countries did not influence the making of the 1975 Agrarian Reform. In fact both the Soviet Union and China had warned that such a radical reform would lead to great instability and the threat of revolution. Undeterred by this warning, the Ethiopians undertook the implementation of the Reform. Hence, the Agrarian Reform in Ethiopia was not to avoid communism, as was the case in many of the land reform programs examined by Tai, but rather it was instituted as part of an attempt to eventually embrace the goals of a communist society. This government objective, however, is mitigated by the unfavorable attitude of peasants towards joining collective forms of production, at present. The implication of the peasants' negative attitude towards collective farming will be examined in the next chapter.

A. Issues Emerging After the Agrarian Reform

The field investigation in Arsi revealed that even after the Agrarian Reform, the effects of land distribution and the peasants' attitudes towards land security are still factors which significantly influence their productivity. Land held by the peasants association is distributed according to three criteria; these are: (A) family size (B) total area under the jurisdiction of a peasant association, and (C) the number of households in a peasant association. The peasant association strives to distribute land among its members in such a way that each family receives an area of equal size and comparable quality. With an annual population increase of 2.8 % and new members periodically entering the association as head of household, the pattern of land distribution changes within a relatively short period of time. Consequently, this issue was addressed during the field work by posing the question of whether or not there had been land adjustment (referred as 2nd stage redistribution by the government) after the initial (first) stage of land distribution in 1975.

Table 4

Land Adjustment in Peasant Association Since the Reform

Land Adjustment in PA Since the Reform	Number Interviewed	Percentage of Total Interviewed
Land Has Been Adjusted in PA	75	50
Land Has Not Been Adjusted in PA	75	50
Total	150	100

Table 4 points out that half of the respondents experienced land redistribution in their peasant association since the first land distribution in 1975. This is an important finding since one of the few field studies conducted after the Agrarian Reform in both the northern and southern regions of Ethiopia indicated that there was very little land redistribution undertaken in peasant associations due to a lack of administrative and technical capability. This lack of redistribution has contributed to inequality in landholding. (27) But in Arsi land redistribution has resulted in relative equality in landholding.

The majority of the respondents (63%) who reported land adjustment in their peasant association lived in Chilalo Awraja. This may be attributed to the integrated programs of CADU/ARDU which may have contributed to better local organization with capable leadership and administration services.

The impact of land redistribution has an adverse impact on the size of landholding . Most of the farmers, 65% whose peasant association has undergone redistribution indicated that their land size had decreased after redistribution. And nearly half of those with a decrease in their land size have reported a decrease in their agricultural output. These findings have a disturbing implication for agricultural productivity. Cultivatable land under peasant farming has expanded more rapidly in Arsi than elsewhere in Ethiopia. Yet, land redistribution since 1976 has meant a decrease in farm size for most peasants. This phenomenon is to be experienced intensely in other regions which have a higher population growth rate and limited potential for land expansion within the peasant association.

The issue being raised does not concern the on-going debate on whether or not farm size has an impact on agricultural production (which will be explained in detail in Chapter 6) but, rather, concerns the impact of redistribution of farm size and productivity. With no improvement in farming technology and a high rate of population growth, diminishing farm size is likely to be an obstacle to agricultural growth in Ethiopia. The government's original intention, that the objective of 2nd stage redistribution would lead to consolidation and collective forms of production, is contrary to the reality of the workings of peasant associations.

Land tenure insecurity, which was found to be a major obstacle to increased peasant production prior to the Agrarian Reform, is still found to be an outstanding issue facing peasant agriculture in Ethiopia. (28) The evaluation report taken in Arsi just before the 1974 revolution stated that "in view of the grave impediment to development caused by insecurity of tenure,...the Imperial Ethiopian Government (should) enact legislation which effectively protects tenancy and (should) enforce the legislation strictly." (29)

Farmers' feelings on land tenure security are presented in Table 5.

Table 5

Respondents' Feelings on Land Tenure Security

Land Tenure Security	No. Interviewed	% of Interviewed
Feel Secure About Long-term Tenure	95	63
Do Not Feel Secure About Long-term Tenure of Land	55	37
Total	150	100

Table 5 indicates that 63% of the sampled farmers in Arsi feel secure about their land. This finding may look surprising at first, given the effort expended by extension agents and political institutions to attract farmers to establish or join collective forms of production in their peasant association. But there remains an adequate explanation for the large percentage of peasants who feel secure about long-term land tenure: to begin with, nearly half of the peasant farmers in Arsi experienced tenancy before the Reform; their present status as landowners (even if they lack private ownership), allows them to enjoy more land security now than before. Secondly, farmers have witnessed the cessation of tenant eviction since the Agrarian Reform, especially in Chilalo. Thirdly, because of their exposure to CADU/ARDU projects and frequent contacts with extension agents, most farmers may be aware of the government policy of voluntaryism; that is, peasants do not feel forced to give up their individual farms and join collective forms of production. Finally, the Reform has created what Dessalegn Rahmato calls "uniformity of tenure" a situation in which peasants enjoy usufruct rights of their farms in a climate of reduced social stratification. (30)

By studying whether or not there is a statistical relationship between the status of farmers before the Agrarian Reform and their degree of land tenure security, an interesting insight can be observed. The majority of former tenants (60%), as well as former owner-cultivators (65%), feel secure about their land. Hence a peasant's previous status does not provide an adequate explanation for his feelings on land security. Yet, further investigation of former tenants and former owner-cultivators who feel secure about their land revealed that a large number of them reported that there had not been land redistribution in their peasant association since the initial one in 1975. Hence, land redistribution, which has frequently led to a decrease in farm size may be a source of land tenure insecurity.

The study shows that the number of former owner-cultivators who feel secure about their land is greater than the number of former tenants feeling the same way; one factor that may have contributed to this disparity is the fact that owner-cultivators live in areas where there are very few producer cooperatives and where there are no strong movements for establishing collective forms of production. The author interviewed an example of such a farmer, a man who lives in Kofelle RDC Chilalo Awraja, in a peasant association of 902 hectares and 206 members. He is a Muslim, 40 years old, with two wives and eight children. He can neither read nor write. He has two hectares of land, which is half the size of the land he cultivated prior to the Agrarian Reform. He cultivates enset (false banana) and barley, mainly for consumption. He owns 35 dairy cattle that serve his family as a source income. He feels secure about the long-term tenure of his land and would like to remain a smallholder. Most farmers in Kofelle are engaged in livestock production and there are very few producer cooperatives in the area. In the two peasant associations covered by this study there was no attempt to establish producer cooperatives.

The establishment of producer cooperatives in a peasant association tends to lead to insecurity in land tenure among those who are not members of the producer cooperative. The chairman of the producer cooperative is usually the chairman of the peasant association. In some instances, where land belonging to smallholders was found to be desirable for collective farming, smallholders could be asked to settle elsewhere in the peasant association, thus placing additional peer pressure on the smallholders to join producer cooperatives. In addition, peasants in both associations in Kofelle indicated that they had not experienced land redistribution since the first one undertaken in 1975. ARDU extension agents who have lived in Kofelle for a number of years seem to agree that there has not been as much land redistribution in this area as compared to the major cereal-producing regions under the control of peasant associations in other parts of Arsi.

The other areas in which most of the owner-cultivators express land tenure security, possess the following attributes in all three Awrajas: they are lowland areas where land is relatively plentiful, where livestock is a major occupation, and where there is very little pressure exerted by government and ARDU agents to establish producer cooperatives because of the agricultural potential of these areas.

Further examination of the respondents who felt insecure about their land tenure revealed useful insights. (Table 6)

Table 6

Primary Reason for Insecurity of Land Tenure

Reason for Land Insecurity	# Interviewed	% Interviewed
Land belongs to the government	22	40
Fears land distribution in peasant association	18	33
Fears peasant association will turn into producer cooperative	10	18
Land belongs to all people	5	9
Total	55	100

A large number of the respondents (40%) who cited land belonging to the government as a reason for their land tenure insecurity were tenants. Given the decisive role that the government played in introducing the Agrarian Reform, it is likely that some peasants maintain the belief that the government can undo the Reform without their consultation. The sentiments of the farmers who gave this response are best expressed by a 50-year-old former tenant who said "land security is as uncertain as the rainy season during "belg" (the short rainy period during the dry season). The rain depends on the will of god and our land on the will of the government."

All of the respondents who feared land size could be altered at the discretion of their peasant association (33%), have experienced land adjustment in their peasant association since the initial distribution resulting in the reduction of their farm size.

Peasant associations also have the authority to move farm families around in order to consolidate the land they deem desirable for producer cooperatives. It was observed that in some instances, when the chairman and some of the executive committee members of peasant association were also in charge of a producer cooperative, peasants expressed their anxiety about being able to keep their farm. They feared that they might be asked to move elsewhere if they wanted like to remain smallholders or else be forced to join producer cooperatives.

Among the respondents who fear that their peasant association may be turned into producer cooperatives (18%), most of them live in Chilalo areas where there is a successful movement to mobilize farmers to join producer cooperatives. The 5 respondents who indicated that land belongs to all people live in Chilalo and are willing to join producer cooperatives when they are formed in their peasant association.

Closely related to the issue of land security is the question of farm investment. In this study farmers were asked whether they had invested in their farm and if so (Table 7), what factors had influenced their investment.

Table 7

Farm Investment After the Agrarian Reform

Farm Investment Since 1975	# Interviewed	% of Interviewed
Have Invested in Farm	67	45
Have not Invested in Farm	83	55
Total	150	100

Those who invested in their farm did so by buying oxen, purchasing farm equipment, building storage and terraces, practicing crop rotation and improving tillage practices, and planting trees. An analysis of the respondents who invested in their farms revealed that 53% reported an increase in the size of their cultivated area, 37% reported a decrease and 10% said their area had remained the same as prior to 1975. Hence, it is likely that an increase in cultivatable land contributes to the desire to make farm investments. In a further probe, over half of the farmers who invested in their farm live in the high cereal-producing regions of Chilalo Awraja, and attributed the idea for such investments to ARDU extension agents. This is because ARDU's extension services have been concentrated on the major grain-producing areas since the early days of the integrated rural development experiments of CADU, and farmers in this region are receptive to innovations and new ideas.

Research on the relationship between land security and farm investment is very limited. One of the few empirical studies in Costa Rica found a positive relationship between land security and improved performance measured in terms of farm investment and output. (31) In general, the Latin American experience suggests that in addition to prices, availability of inputs, access to markets, farmers' awareness of opportunity, and land tenure security are acknowledged to be powerful incentives for increased farm investment, which in turn leads to increased production. (32)

In an attempt to determine whether or not there is a relationship between investing in one's farm and possessing a feeling of land security, the two were cross-tabulated. (Table 8)

Table 8

Relationship Between Farm Investment and Land Tenure Security

Investment since Reform	Feel Secure	Don't Feel Secure	# of Cases
Have Invested	85%	15%	67
Have Not Made Investment	46%	54%	83

Chi Square 23 significant at 0.05 level and beyond

Table 8 shows that 85% of the farmers who have made some investment in their land feel secure about the long-term tenure of their land. In further examination of these respondents, approximately 40% were former tenants whose cultivated area, as well as their agricultural production, had increased since the Agrarian Reform. Therefore, the conclusion of the study is the following: what has happened to the size of cultivated area since the Reform affects dramatically the farmer's feeling of land security, thereby influencing his desire to invest in the farm and eventually determining the rate of productivity of that farm.

44

Notes

1. Peter Dorner and Don Kanel, "The Economic Case for Land Reform: Employment, Income Distribution and Productivity: Issues and Cases," in *Land Reform in Latin America*, Edited by Peter Dorner, Madison: University of Wisconsin, Madison, 1971, pp. 41-56.

2. Some of the most important writings on land reform are: Alain de Janvry, *The Agrarian Question and Reformism in Latin America*, Baltimore: The John Hopkins University Press, 1981.

Kieth Griffin, *The Political Economy of Agrarian Change*, London: The MacMillian Press LTD, 1979;

Russel King, *Land Reform: A World Survey*, Boulder, Colorado: Westview Press, 1977;

Jeffery M. Paige, *Agrarian Revolution: Social Movements and Export Agriculture in Underdeveloped World*, New York: The Free Press, 1975;

Hung-Choi Tai, *Land Reform and Politics: A Comparative Analysis*, Berkley: University of California Press, 1974;

Elisa H. Tuma, *Twenty-Six Centuries of Agrarian Reform: A Comparative Analysis*, Berkeley: University of California Press, 1965;

Louis J. Walinsky, *Agrarian Reform as Unfinished Business*, London: Oxford University Press, 1977.

3. Russell King, *Land Reform: A World Survey*, Boulder, Colorado: Westview Press, 1977, p. 14; and Hung-Choi Tai, *Land Reform and Politics: A Comparative Analysis*, Berkley: University of California Press, 1974, pp. 11-12.

4. Ajit Kuma Ghose, *Agrarian Reform in Contemporary Developing Countries*, New York: St. Martin Press, 1983, p. 5.

5. *IBID*, P. 6

6. Mahtama Sellassie W/Meskel, "Land Tenure and Taxation from Ancient to Modern Times," *Ethiopia Observer 4*, No. 5 (1964); See also

Allan Hoben, *Land Tenure Among the Amhare of Ethiopia: The Dynamic of Cognitive Descent*, Chicago: University of Chicago Press, 1973;

Patrik Gilkes, *The Dying Lion: Feudalism and Modernization in Ethiopia*, London: Julian Friedman, 1975.

7. Joanna Mantel-Niecko, *The Role of Land Tenure in the System of Ethiopian Imperial Government in Modern Times*, Warsaw: University of Warsaw, 1980.

8. *IBID*, pp. 204-205.

9. Dessalegn Rahmato, *Agrarian Reform in Ethiopia*, Uppsala: Scandinavian Institute of African Studies, 1984; and see also

H.C. Dunning, " Land Reform In Ethiopia: A Case Study in Non-development," *U.C.L.A. Law Review, XVIII,2, 1970;*

Asefa Bequel and Eshetu Chole, *A Profile of the Ethiopian Economy*, Addis Ababa: Oxford University Press, 1969;

Gene Ellis, "The Feudal Paradigm as a Hindrance to Understanding Ethiopia," *The Journal of Modern African Studies*,14,2, 1976, pp. 275-295;

Zultan Gyenge, *Ethiopia on the Road of Non-capitalist Development*, Budapest: Studies of Developing Countries, Paper No. 90, 1976.

10. *Report on the Land Tenure Survey of Arussi Province*, Ministry of Land Reform and Administration, Addis Ababa, 1976, p. 22.

11. Henock Kiefle, *An Analysis of the CADU Credit Program 1968/69 to 1970/71 and its Impact on Income Distribution*, Asella, CADU Publication No. 66, 1971.

12. *CADU General Agricultural Survey*, 1970, CADU Publication No. 71, Assella, 1971, p. 6.

13. David Lehman, "The Death of Land Reform: A Polemic," *World Development*, Volume 6, No. 3, 1978, pp. 339-345.

14. John K. Galbraith, "Conditions of Economic Change in Under-Developed Countries," *Journal of Farm Economics*, XLIII, November 1951, p. 695.

15. Alain de Janvry, *The Agrarian Question and Reformism in Latin America*, Baltimore: The John Hopkins University Press, 1981, pp. 202-211.

16. *IBID*, pp. 211-223.

17. Allan Hoben, "Perspectives on Land Reform in Ethiopia: The Political Role of the Peasantry," *Rural Africana*, No. 28, edited by John Harbeson and Paul Brietzke, East Lansing: Michigan State University, 1975, p. 79.

18. Marina Ottoway, "Land Reform in Ethiopia 1974-1977," *The African Studies Review*, Volume XX, No. 3, December 1977, p. 79.

19. Allan Hoben, "Perspectives on Land Reform in Ethiopia: The Political Role of the Peasantry." *Rural Africana* No. 28, edited by John Harbeson and Paul Brietzke, East Lansing: Michigan State University, 1975, pp. 63-67; see also

Alula Abate and Fassil G. Kiros, "Agrarian Reform, Structural Change, and Rural Development in Ethiopia," in Ajit Kuma Ghose, *Agrarian Reform in Contemporary Developing Countries*, New York: St. Martin Press, 1983, pp. 160-164.

20. Marina Ottoway, "Land Reform and Peasant Association: Preliminary Analysis," *Rural Africana*, No. 28, edited by John Harbeson and Paul Brietzke, East Lansing: Michigan State University, 1975, p. 48. See also

Allan Hoben, "Perspectives on Land Reform in Ethiopia: The Political Role of the Peasantry," *Rural Africana*, No. 28, edited by John Harbeson and Paul Brietzke, East Lansing: Michigan State University, 1975,pp. 66-68.

21. On the implementation of the reform see: Alula Abate and Fassil G. Kiros, " Agrarian Reform, Structural Change, and Rural Development in

46

Ethiopia," in Ajit Kuma Ghose, *Agrarian Reform in Contemporary Developing Countries*, New York: St. Martin Press, 1983, pp. 154-164.;

Paul Brietzke," Land Reform in Revolutionary Ethiopia," *The Journal of Modern African Study*, Volume 14, December 1976, No. 4, pp. 637-660;

Marina Ottoway "Land Reform and Peasant Association: Preliminary Analysis," *Rural Africana*, No. 28, edited by John Harbeson and Paul Brietzke, East Lansing: Michigan State University, 1975, pp. 39-54 ; and

Marina and David Ottoway, *Ethiopia: Empire in Revolution*, New York: African Publishing Company, 1978, pp. 71-78.

22. Ministry of Agriculture, *Ke Yekatit isk Yekatit*, Addis Ababa: Ethiopia, 1984.

23. Land Reform: Land Settlements and Cooperatives. *Rome: Food and Agricultural Organization of the United Nations*, No. 1/2, 1981, p. 37.

24. Hung-Choi Tai, *Land Reform and Politics: A Comparative Analysis*, Berkley: University of California Press, 1974, p. 7.

25. *IBID*, pp. 324-463.

26. Adrian Wood, "Rural Development and Integration in Ethiopia," *African Affairs*, Volume 82, No. 329, Oct. 1983, pp. 528-535.

27. Alula Abate and Tesfaye Teklu, "Land Reform and Peasant Association in Ethiopia: Case Studies from Two Widely Differing Regions," *Northeast African Studies*, 2,2, 1980. pp. 30-47.

28. *Review of Arsi Rural Development Unit*, Stockholm: Sweden, SIDA, January 1985, pp. 9- 11.

29. Guy Hunter et al, *Final Report of the Appraisal of CADU and EPID*, Stockholm, Sweden: 1974, p. 82.

30. Dessalegn Rahmato, *Agrarian Reform in Ethiopia*, Uppsala: Scandinavian Institute of African Studies, 1984, p. 62.

31. Sallas Oscar, Foster Knight and Calos Saenza, *Land Tilling in Costa Rica: A Legal and Economic Survey*, San Jose: University of Costa Rica, 1970.

32. Joseph R. Thame,"Improving Land Tenure Security," in *Land Reform in Latin America,Issues and Cases*, edited by Peter Dorner, Madison: University of Wisconsin, 1971, pp. 229-257.

Chapter 4

The Role of Peasant Institutions in Socialist Transformation and Rural Development

The 1975 Rural Land Proclamation in Ethiopia triggered the emergence of peasant institutions, based on socialist principles, that were intended to bring about the political, economic, and social transformation of rural Ethiopia. The first institution to be founded at that time was the peasant association. Soon every peasant association was required to form a women's association. In 1978, when the Ethiopian Revolution took a decisive step and introduced "*scientific socialism,*" it gave directions for the establishment of service cooperatives and producer cooperatives; structures which are meant to serve as instruments for the socialist transformation of the peasant sector. The functions of these institutions, their performance and the peasant's attitudes towards them will be examined in this chapter.

I. The Peasant Association:

Prior to the Agrarian Reform, the Ethiopian peasantry lived in scattered homesteads and had no effective network to promote or protect its political and economic interests. This state of disorganization was seen as a major hindrance to the attainment of higher productivity among peasant farmers. The establishment of peasant associations was the most vital step undertaken to overcome the structural problems of peasant production.

The institution which best symbolizes the Agrarian Reform in Ethiopia is the peasant association, which has been the foundation of rural life since the March 4, 1975 Rural Land Proclamation. (1) The proclamation (proclamation No. 31) gave a specific mandate for peasant associations to undertake the following tasks:

1. to distribute land as equitably as possible;
2. to follow land use directives issued by the government;
3. to administer and conserve public property within the area;
4. to establish judicial tribunals for land disputes;
5. to establish marketing and credit cooperatives and women's and youth associations;
6. to build schools, clinics, and to provide other social services needed in the area;
7. to cultivate the holdings of persons who by reason of age or health are unable to cultivate their holding; and
8. to encourage villagization.

The degree to which these functions are undertaken successfully by the peasant association varies from one region to another depending on its administrative capacity, peasant consciousness and the support it receives from government agencies. The most important task that was satisfactorily undertaken by the majority of peasant associations, regardless of region, is the distribution of land to members. In Arsi, however, self-help activities (such as building schools, clinics and rural roads) and cooperative development are the dominant concern that occupy peasant associations. This can be explained in part by the higher political awareness of the peasants in this region who have experienced tenancy; other factors involved are the adverse impact of mechanization and the active participation of ARDU extension agents in assisting the peasant association to undertake such activities.

The proclamation, on the whole, indicates the government's intention to establish peasant associations as autonomous law-and-order units promoting the social, economic and political development of peasants within a specific area. The reason for the government's emphasis on autonomy has been intensely debated. But it seems that it has to do more with the government's ideological commitment than with its inability to control the process of peasant association formation; at least this is true for the early stages of the Ethiopian Revolution.

Following the proclamation, many students believed that peasant associations would emerge as a force opposing the military government. As pointed out by Marina Ottoway, who had observed the process of peasant association formation, the presence of a large number of students in the country-side (deployed in the "Development Through Cooperation Campaign"), the collapse of the previous administrative structure, and peasant enthusiasm for land reform are factors that would have encouraged peasant associations to become a force antagonistic to the government. (2) As important as these factors were, particularly in the first few months of the land reform, the peasant associations did not present a formidable challenge to the military government.

The students gained the support of the peasantry in their fight against the former landlords and elites. Inexperienced in mass organization and doctrinaire in their approach, they attempted to impose a Chinese-style communism on the peasantry. This caused the initial support the students enjoyed from the peasantry to dwindle. Peasants, by in large, began to resent the students' authoritarian attitude towards them, their undue intervention in the running of the peasant association and their relentless push for collective forms of production. The student-led unrest in many parts of the country brought military intervention. The government no longer left the process of peasant association formation to the students and the peasants, since they realized it would mean the spread of anarchy in the countryside. The government appointed new Awraja and Wereda-level administrators to fill the vacuum created by the the fall of the previous government and assigned Land Reform Officers in each Wereda to advise on the implementation of the Reform. During the confrontation between the students and the government, the peasants decisively took the side of the government, supporting the gradual change which they considered to be to their advantage. Hence, the peasant association as a force opposing government authority did not materialize.

To clarify some of the ambiguities of the March 4, 1975 Proclamation regarding peasant association autonomy, the government issued a complementary proclamation ten months later, in December 14, 1975 called "The Peasant Association and Consolidation Proclamation" (Proclamation #71). This proclamation gave peasant associations legal personalities as well as rights to establish cooperative societies which would serve as a basis for socialist agriculture. It also created an administrative structure, at each Wereda level, known as "The Revolutionary Administration and Development Committee," to integrate peasant associations into the regional administration. This committee is composed of local government officials, political cadres, Ministry of Agriculture Officers or extension agents at the Wereda level, and representatives of peasant associations. The structural linkage between the Wereda level Revolutionary Administrative and Development Committee and the peasant associations has its benefits and shortcomings. On the one hand, it enables peasant associations to coordinate their activities and receive assistance from the government. On the other hand, it could be used by the government to impose its agenda on the peasantry and interfere in the activities of the peasant association. In reality, the proclamation has undoubtedly given more autonomy to the peasant association. It has simultaneously established grassroots organizations that could effectively be used to promote government programs.

A. The Administration of Peasant Associations

Peasant associations in most areas have assumed the responsibility of local government at the village level as envisioned in the proclamation. The main administrative organs of the peasant association (referred to as the "leading organ" by the government) are the general assembly, the executive committee, the inspection committee, the judicial committee and the defense committee.

The general assembly consists of all head-of-households in the peasant association. In principle, it is the highest decision-making body and is in charge of appointing and removing people in the administrative organs of the peasant association. In practice, however, it is weaker, less cohesive, and less influential than the executive committee which it appoints. This is partly because peasants in most regions have not fully realized the kind of power they could exercise through their peasant association and partly because of the authoritarian attitude exhibited by members of the executive committee and local government officials towards the peasant. Some government officials' condescending attitude towards peasants is remarkably similar to the attitude existing between the power class and the poor in feudal Ethiopia.

One of the few field studies in this area was conducted by Dessalegn Rahmato, who examined the internal workings of peasant associations. His study found that the general assembly is manipulated by the executive committee and local government officials. He argues that the general assembly is used as "rubber stamp to endorse decisions or approve measures already taken." (3) This observation may accurately reflect the situation in many regions of Ethiopia. But the field investigation in Arsi revealed the general assembly to be a much more active body in making decisions than what was observed in Dessalegn study. In fact, the general assembly asserted its power over the executive committee and over outside influences as much as possible. The majority of the sampled farmers in this study (79%) indicated that they are involved in the decision-making process in their peasant association. This was also confirmed by the chairmen of most of the sampled peasant associations who reported that at least two-thirds of the members of the general assembly have to be present for a binding decision to be made or approved by the peasant association. There were also instances in both the Chilalo and Ticho Awrajas where the general assembly voted to unseat the chairman and the treasurer because of alleged use of the peasant association fund for private purposes. However, this is not to suggest that the executive committee in Arsi is less powerful than the general assembly, but rather the power of the executive committee is mitigated by the high level of peasant participation in the general assembly.

The executive committee is by far the most powerful and influential organ. It is a cohesive body that meets more regularly than the general assembly. It consists of a chairman, a treasurer and secretary who oversee the daily activities of the association. It appoints a sub-committee to promote and supervise production, education and self-help activities. The executive officers, particularly the chairman of the peasant association, works closely with government officials, extension agents, and are members of the Revolutionary Administration and Development Committee at the Wereda level. This connection provides the executive officers with access to government channels, thereby making them even more powerful and highly influential *vis-a-vis* the general assembly. The revolutionary defense committee, which both enforces law and order and protects peasants' interest from "anti-revolutionary elements," is under the control of the executive committee. In most cases, the executive committee elects members of the revolutionary defense committee and then seeks the approval of the general assembly.

The judicial committee, consisting of a three man tribunal, settles land disputes and criminal offenses against other members of the peasant association. In Arsi most peasant associations keep a record of disputes, particularly disputes of a criminal nature. But in other regions of Ethiopia very few records are kept because of the low level of literacy in the judicial committee. The judicial committee has the authority to fine offenders up to 300 birr and three months imprisonment in the peasant association jail.

Such judicial tribunals, whose members are elected by the constituency of the peasant association, are maintained at the Wereda and Awraja administrative levels. This court system, which functions apart from the government's Ministry of Justice has, profoundly changed the legal system in Ethiopia. The system not only gives peasants direct access to the court at the village level (and appeal at the Wereda level if they are dissatisfied with the ruling) but it also provides peasant associations with the legal rights to decide on land distribution and other issues without interference from government agencies. Hence, under the present legal structure, peasant associations have the potential to influence government policy and undertake peasant-organized planning and development.

In 1982 the government introduced the Inspection Committee, an investigative unit designed to be one of the "leading organs" of the peasant association. The inspection Committee acts as an overseer to the elected officers and monitors the activities of the peasant association. In Arsi, two instances were observed in which the Inspection Committee brought charges of favoritism and corruption against a member of the executive committee, eventually leading to their dismissal. The Inspection Committee has the potential to serve as a system of checks and balances to the enormous power the executive committee wields. At present, most peasants and their leaders are unclear about the role and the power of the Inspection Committee *vis-a-vis* the other organs of the peasant association.

Peasant associations are organized in a hierarchy from the lowest village level, called Kebelle Peasant Associations, to the highest national level, known as the All Ethiopian Peasant Association (AEPA). Peasant associations at the Kebelle level elect their representative to the Wereda committee; the Wereda representative elects those to serve at the Awraja level; the Awraja committee elects those who will serve at the regional level; and the regional office selects representatives to the All Ethiopian Peasant Association general assembly. This institutional network has firmly established peasant associations as a mass organization outside of the government bureaucracy. But at the same time, the government uses this network to reach peasants to carry out its own programs. The government administrative structure extends only to the Wereda level and therefore has to use Kebelle-level peasant associations to reach peasants at the grassroots level.

The single most important function of peasant associations is the distribution, redistribution, and management of land. This is a continuous process that takes a great deal of time; land has to be adjusted to accommodate new members, a change in family size or an alteration in the quality of land within the peasant association's holdings.

Peasant associations are currently joining hands to undertake self-help schemes such as building schools, clinics and rural roads. This is particularly true in Arsi, where the dominant issues that increasingly occupy the peasant association are mobilizing resources for development activities and cooperative promotion.

Among the sampled farmers in Arsi, 91% of them attributed the level of improvement in literacy to the adult literacy campaign which was organized by their peasant association; 89% said that being a member of the peasant association has provided them access to credit which they never had before; nearly all of them showed unwavering loyalty to their peasant association, equating its foundation with the abolishment of the previous feudal order.

B. Factors Affecting Peasant Association Functions

This study found that the most significant issues facing peasant associations are (1) variation in the number of members and the size of land in the peasant association and, (2) leadership and the relationship between the peasant association and the government agencies. These issues will increasingly affect the potential of the peasant association to be an autonomous local organization as well as a self-sufficient production unit.

1. Size and Membership in a Peasant Association:

The proclamation of 1975 stated the ideal size of a peasant association to be 800 ha. with 275 households. Studies from several regions of Ethiopia indicate that, contrary to what the government expected, the size and membership of peasant associations vary widely. One of the first field studies undertaken two years after the land reform in Shashemena Wereda, Shewa region, (250 kilometers away from Addis Ababa) showed that the size of peasant associations ranged from 400 to 840 ha. (with an average size of 640 ha.) and that membership ranged from 130 to 485. (4) A more extensive study involving 20 highland peasant associations in ten administrative regions was completed in 1983. This study indicated that the size of the peasant associations ranged from 240 ha. to 1600 ha. (with an average size of 932 ha.) and that membership ranged from 205 to 2050 (with an average membership of 576 farm families). (5)

In this study 30 peasant associations from the highland, medium altitude and lowland zones were randomly selected. Their size, membership, and density is presented in Table 9.

Table 9

Size, Membership, and Density of Sampled Peasant Association in Arsi

Size of PA (HA)	# of Households	Awraja	Ecological Zone	Density (Area in ha. per household)
437	107	Chilalo	Highland	4.1
520	134	Arbagugu	Highland	3.9
560	260	Chilalo	Medium Altitude	2.2
640	167	Chilalo	Medium Altitude	3.8
640	319	Chilalo	Medium Altitude	3.8
680	169	Arbagugu	Lowland	4.0
800	102	Chilalo	Lowland	7.8
800	135	Arbagugu	Lowland	5.9
800	164	Chilalo	Lowland	4.9
800	179	Chilalo	Highland	4.5
800	230	Ticho	Medium Altitude	3.5
800	402	Ticho	Medium Altitude	2.0
880	280	Chilalo	Medium Altitude	3.1
880	280	Ticho	Highland	3.1
880	347	Arbagugu	Medium Altitude	2.5
885	190	Arbagugu	Medium Altitude	4.7
900	268	Chilalo	Highland	3.4
902	206	Chilalo	Highland	4.4
920	278	Chilalo	Highland	3.3
930	203	Arbagugu	Medium Altitude	4.6
1000	245	Chilalo	Highland	4.1
1000	249	Chilalo	Highland	4.0
1000	263	Arbagugu	Highland	3.8
1000	280	Chilalo	Highland	3.6
1000	299	Chilalo	Highland	3.3
1000	342	Ticho	Medium Altitude	2.9
1100	309	Ticho	Medium Altitude	3.6
120	232	Chilalo	Highland	4.8
1200	248	Chilalo	Lowland	4.9

Table 9 shows that the size of peasant associations ranged from 437 ha. to 1,200 ha., membership from 102 to 402 households, and density from 2 ha. to 7.8 ha. per household in Arsi. The smallest peasant association with an area of 437 ha. is found in the highland zone near Asella, in Chilalo Awraja. The largest peasant association is also in Chilalo, in the lowland areas of Dhera RDC. The most sparsely populated peasant association, with 102 households, and the most densely populated peasant association, with 402 members, both cover 800 ha. The former is located in the lowlands of Chilalo and the latter in the fertile medium altitude of Ticho Awraja. In sum, there is a wide difference in size and membership among the sampled peasant associations in Arsi, many of which do not correspond to the government-legislated ideal size. The following factors are likely to contribute to such disparity.

First, there was a local social institution peculiar to Arsi prior to 1975 known as Golmassa. Its function was to assist in promoting law and order and in collecting taxes and demographic data. It usually covered an area of 800 ha. However, in areas that were densely populated, the size was less than 800 ha. and in areas that were sparsely populated, there were large uncultivated areas of more than 800 ha. It is likely that most Golmassas were converted into peasant associations and, as a result, have maintained the previous variation in size and membership of the Golmassas. In fact, it is rumored that the Golmassa may have inspired the land reform since there was no other precedent of a rural institution with an ideal size of 800 ha. in other regions of Ethiopia.

Second, the Agrarian Reform was enthusiastically embraced by the overwhelming majority of peasant farmers in Arsi as well as in many other regions of Ethiopia where tenancy was widespread. Its implementation, including the formation of peasant associations was carried out with great speed. No careful measurement or surveying of the area was done when the boundaries of the peasant associations were established. Students participating in the "Development through Cooperative Campaign" were responsible for the guidance of peasants during the formation of the peasant associations. These students have very little knowledge of surveying methods, measurements and the particular setting of the area. This may have contributed to the variation in the size of peasant associations.

Third, the Rural Land Proclamation established the rights of tenants to remain on the land they were cultivating. This had the unintended outcome of discouraging farmers from claiming land in the sparsely populated regions outside their area. Most farmers preferred to stay in the area they were cultivating even if there was a possibility of getting a larger land-holding in another peasant association with which they were unfamiliar. This assertion seem to be supported by the findings of this study which suggest that 73% of evicted tenants claimed the same land they had cultivated prior to eviction.

Fourth, it appears that the formation of peasant associations was partly a reflection of the traditional boundaries and kinship patterns of the rural society in Arsi. Peasants, for the most part, did not consider land population ratios or ecological variation when establishing peasant associations. An example of this kind of oversight was observed in Ticho Awraja where a peasant association is comprised of both medium altitude and lowland zones. Farming activities and size of landholdings differ between the two zones. Farmers in the medium altitude zone grow cereals and have smaller holdings than those in the lowlands, where most raise livestock and have larger holdings. This phenomenon was also observed in Chilalo Awraja, Dhera RDC. In both cases, loyalty to the historical ties among the people was given precedence over differing farming practices and ecological zones when the peasant association were formed.

Fifth, the number of farm families in the peasant association seems to be greatly influenced by fertility. Using density as an indicator (farm size/ household) as indicated in Table 9, the density of peasant associations in the lowland averages 5.5, in the highland 3.8 , and in the medium altitude zone 3.2. This suggests that peasant associations in the medium altitude and highland zones, which have relatively fertile land and have a higher potential for cereal production, are more densely populated than the lowland areas.

Because of the wide range in density among peasant associations, a statistical test was done to find whether or not there is a relationship between the size and membership of a peasant association and ecological zone (see Tables 10 and 11). For statistical reasons, the size of the peasant associations shown in Table 9 were put into four categories: (a) 400 to 700 ha., (b) 701 to 900 ha., (c) 901 to 1000 ha., and (d) 1001 1200 ha. Peasant associations were also divided into four groups by number of households: (a) 100 to 150, (B) 151 to 200, (c) 201 to 300 and (d) 301 to 402 households.

Table 10

Relationship Between ARDU Ecological Zones and Size of Peasant Association

Ecological zone	400-700	701-900	901-1000	1001-1200	# of cases
Highland	23%	30%	40%	7%	71
Medium Altitude.	30%	35%	18%	17%	54
Lowland	15%	55%	5%	25%	25

chi square 30.3 significant at 0.05 level and beyond (6 degree of freedom).

The cross-tabulation in Table 10 shows a statistically significant relationship between the size of the peasant association and ecological zones. Of the respondents who lived in the smallest peasant association (400 to 700 ha.) the largest number belonged in medium altitude (30%) and highland zones (23%). In the largest peasant associations (1001 to 1200 ha.), the largest number of the respondents (25%) lived in the lowland zone. In general, the respondents who lived in the highland and medium altitudes, belong to associations with smaller landholdings.

Table 11

Relationship Between ARDU Ecological Zone and Number of Households in a Peasant Association

Ecological Zone	Number of Households in a Peasant Association				
	100-150	151-200	201-300	301-402	# of Cases
Highland	14%	7%	70%	9%	71
Medium Altitude	0%	19%	46%	35%	54
Lowland	40%	40%	5%	15%	25

Chi Square 62.3 significant at 0.05 level and beyond (6 degrees of freedom).

Among the respondents who live in the highlands, 70% belong to a peasant association that has a membership of 201 to 301 households; among those in the medium altitude, 46% belong in this category, and there are 5% in the lowland zone who belong in this category. A large number of the respondents (80%) live in the sparsely populated peasant associations which have 100 to 200 members, whereas only 20% live in the densely populated peasant associations which have 200 to 400 members. Thus, the findings in Table 11 suggest that peasant associations in the highland and medium altitude are more densely populated than those in the lowland zone. This is because the highland and medium altitude are more fertile and well-adapted to cereal cultivation than the lowland zone. As a result, it is likely that there will be over-cultivation, over-crowding, and over-grazing that would affect soil fertility. This is a major problem seen in the famine stricken Northern regions of Ethiopia.

The preliminary findings from Table 10 and Table 11 pose a critical policy question regarding peasant production: Does increasing membership in peasant associations in the fertile areas of the highlands and medium altitude adversely affect agricultural production in the long run? There has not been an expansion in the size of peasant associations or any marked improvement in the level of technology since the Agrarian Reform. In addition, the problems of over-cultivation, over-grazing and deforestation plague many parts of the high cereal-producing areas of Arsi.

The effects of these problems were witnessed during the field survey in three peasant associations, all in the fertile medium altitude zones. Two of the peasant associations were found in Chilalo Awraja (one in Degaga RDC with 640 ha. and 319 households and the other in Etheya RDC with 560 ha. and 260 households) and another in Ticho Awraja (with a peasant association size of 800 ha. and 402 households). The average size of the three peasant associations is 666 ha. with 327 members. This size is considerably lower than the average sample size for Arsi of 866 ha. and higher than the average membership of 240 families in a peasant assocation. It varies also from the legislated average of 800 ha. and 275 families.

The size of land available to members in the above mentioned peasant associations is considerably lower as compared to peasant associations in lowland, highland, and even other medium altitude zones (3.2 ha./household). The average cultivated area of members in the three peasant associations is 1.5 ha. whereas 2 ha. is the average holding for the entire sample group in Arsi. Needless to say, these figures confirm the views of farmers and peasant association leaders who indicated during interviews that they are experiencing over-crowding, intensive cultivation, serious shortage of pasture land and land parcelization.

Nearly all of the farmers in the three peasant associations no longer practice periodic fallowing as they used to. This is likely to lead to a decline in soil fertility, given that the amount of fertilizer being used has not increased with their intensive cultivation. As population grows and peasant association in the fertile regions support an increasing number of members, enormous pressure is put on the land to undergo consistent cultivation, and to provide grazing and wood for fuel. If this trend continues unabated, it is reasonable to assume that most peasant associations in the surplus cereal-producing regions will reach an undesirable land/population ratio (both in terms of human and animal populations) that could result in ecological degradation and may, in the long run, even affect rainfall patterns.

This phenomenon in its most extreme form has greatly contributed to the ecological impoverishment of the famine-stricken northern regions of Ethiopia.

Thus, it is important for peasant associations to conform to the ideal size legislated by the government, particularly those in the fertile regions. If adjustments are not made, a devastating land/population ratio could occur and the law of the diminishing marginal return, both in terms of productivity and the condition of the environment, could become a reality in the immediate future. The imminence of this imbalance underlies the importance of involving peasant associations in national planning.

2. Leadership:

Another important finding of this study is the role of leadership in the functioning of peasant association. After reviewing the literature on peasant associations in other regions of Ethiopia, and after observing those in the northern Shoa region which are considered to be strong peasant associations, it is reasonable to say that peasant associations in Arsi are more developed than those of most regions of Ethiopia. They are more active in undertaking development activities and have assumed the functions of local government as envisioned by the Rural Land Proclamation. The success of peasant associations in Arsi is partly due to the able and committed leadership which has gained the respect of peasants as well as the Wereda-level government administrators.

Some of the few field studies in other regions of Ethiopia on this issue have shown that there is widespread corruption, favoritism, mismanagement and turn over in peasant leadership, all of which pose serious obstacles to the smooth functioning of peasant associations. As a result, peasants are less enthusiastic about their peasant associations, less involved in their activities and more resigned to their own impotence to influence events. (6)

Contrary to the above findings, the cases of reported corruption involving the leadership of peasant associations were remarkably few in Arsi. In fact, 76% of the sampled peasants were satisfied with the performance and the leadership of the executive committee and 84% felt that they were actively participating in the decision-making process of their peasant associations. There were also very few instances of the removal of elected officers before the end of their two-year term because they had been accused of corruption, or because they had fallen out of favor with members of other political cadres or government officials.

Favoritism in land distribution, which is alleged to be widespread in many parts of Ethiopia, was rarely reported by peasants or rural development agents in Arsi. Out of the 30 sampled peasant associations, only one reported a case in which there was strong evidence to support peasant allegations of gross inequality in land distribution because of nepotism among the leadership. This peasant association was found in Arbagugu Awraja, in the fertile area of high agricultural potential in Arboye RDC. Most of the sampled farmers interviewed in this peasant association were dissatisfied with executive committee members. When examining the size of cultivated area, this peasant association showed inequality of landholding among the sampled farmers. (Table 12)

Table 12

Comparison of Family Size and Landholding in a Peasant Association

Size of PA (Ha)	# member in PA	Family Size	Cultivated Area (Ha.)
930	203	4	1.5
930	203	5	2.5
930	203	6	1.5
930	203	8	2.0
930	203	8	8.0

Table 12 shows inequalities in the landholding of the farmers in the peasant association accused of corruption in land distribution. Family size is the basic criterion in land distribution. Yet, Table 12 reveals that two farmers with the same size family (8 members) have a wide difference in the size of their culti-vated area - one has 2 ha. and the other has 8 ha. Also, a farmer with a family size of 6 members has the same size of landholding (1.5 ha.) as the one with 4 family members. Thus, Table 12 provides a useful insight into the allegation of favoritism and nepotism in this particular peasant association in Arbagugu.

Further interviews with chairmen and extension agents familiar with this peasant association were conducted. These interviews indicated that the chair-man and the treasurer of this peasant association had been changed four times within the past two years because of proven corruption. This was the highest turn-over among executive members experienced in Arsi; it crippled the admin-istration of the peasant association. There were also a larger number of former landlords and well-to-do peasants in leadership positions. Very few self-help activities were being carried out. This was uncharacteristic of most peasant as-sociations in Arsi where the leadership is dominated by former small owner-cultivators and tenants and a great many self-help activities are undertaken with little outside assistance.

The author discussed the issue of corruption with sampled farmers, selected extension agents and members of the Wereda Revolutionary and Development Committee, an organization that works closely with, supervises, and conducts in-depth examinations of peasant associations accused of corruption. All sug-gested that leadership is a crucial factor in creating a more efficient, better man-agement and administration of peasant associations. The peasants' trust in their leaders is most likely to contribute to a greater participation of members in the decision-making process, in the general assembly as well as in the development activities carried out by the peasant association. Therefore, cultivating capable and committed leaders of peasant associations is an important activity and is necessary if peasant associations are to contribute meaningfully to the transformation of the rural sector in Ethiopia.

II. Women's Associations

Ethiopian women are vital constituents of the socio-economic fabric of the society. In addition to their domestic duties, rural women perform important agricultural and livestock tasks. As observed in Arsi, some women are also involved in household decision-making. Yet, their participation in development projects is extremely low.

The Ethiopian Civil Code, the *Fetah Negest*, stipulated the subordinate position of women in Ethiopian society. According to the *Fetah Negest*, the husband is the head of the family and the wife, who is perceived to be weak and to require male protection, owes him full obedience. The law entitled only men to be registered land-owners and women were effectively excluded from land ownership, except those who were widows.

The 1974 Ethiopian Revolution acknowledged the oppressive legal, economic, cultural and social conditions under which women lived. The government tried to redress these conditions through the 1975 Rural Land Proclamation. The proclamation was progressive with respect to women's issues; it stated that everyone is entitled to cultivate land regardless of sex and calls for equal allocation of land among farm families *where possible*. In practice, this language is ambiguous and has provided loopholes for those peasant associations that do not want to give equal land to women. In all, the distributional effects of the proclamation are mitigated by the ambiguity of the legal reality.

In December 1975, the Ethiopian government took a concrete step to improve conditions for women and to encourage their active involvement in national development. It amended the initial proclamation (through Proclamation No. 71), which authorized peasant associations to establish sister organizations called women's associations. Like peasant associations, women's associations are legally entitled to enter into contracts, to draw their own regulations governing their own association and establish teams that monitor the condition of its members. A women's association is organized in the same way as a peasant association and elects its own officials.

The peasant associations have played a critical role in establishing women's associations. They have assisted women's association leaders to overcome constraints due to their illiteracy and their lack of experience in organizational and administrative matters. Consequently, women's associations have multiplied throughout Ethiopia in a short period of time. In Arsi, for example, every peasant association has a women's association. Nonetheless, the dominance of the peasant association has at times adversely affected the development of the women's association as an autonomous unit.

The findings from this study, as well as those of one of the few studies undertaken by Hanna Kebede on issues of women's associations, reveals that the existing relationship between peasant and women's associations constrains the effective participation of rural women in development. It also hampers their involvement in decision-making concerning their own household and community for the following reasons:

1. Women have only indirect membership in the peasant association through their husband. The only exceptions are widows and co-wives of Muslim families who register as a head of household in a peasant association. The entirely male-dominated peasant association makes all of the major economic and social decisions which affect the community and the farm households. Women's association leaders are not consulted in such decisions.

2. The women's association relies on the peasant association for guidance. Peasant association leaders tend to emphasize the domestic role of women in their programs. This emphasis was also observed by Hanna Kebede who reported that even when women's associations have raised substantial savings, the peasant association pressures them to undertake activities restricted to food preparation, cotton spinning and sewing.(7)

3. Peasant associations have the sole authority to allocate land and labor to the women's association's cooperative farm. Women usually grow vegetables on the cooperative farm to generate income for their association. Not all peasant associations give land to women's association. In some cases, the land given to the women's association is found to be too small and, therefore, their land is less productive. Hanna Kebede's study points out that the labor exchange between peasant and women's associations is often inequitable. The peasant association ploughs the women's cooperative farm. In exchange, the women's association provides labor for weeding, harvesting, food preparation and water provision; a series of tasks which, altogether, are more time consuming. (8)

4. Most women farmers interviewed during the field survey were indifferent about their membership in the women's association. They felt that it distracted them from their household chores and did not like paying membership fees. They perceived the women's association as subordinate to the peasant association and as possessing no influence on the final decisions made for the community. It seems clear that unless women see some measurable benefits, such as increased income or improvement in services (like access to water that will make it easier to do their household chores) women's associations

will be overshadowed by the more visible benefits of being a member of a peasant association.

The dominance of the peasant association over the women's association is largely due to lack of able leadership on the part of the latter. Some of the leaders of women's associations felt that they should at all times support and follow the directives of the peasant association. As one women's association officer put it, "The leaders of peasant associations know better." Hence, training women's association leaders and building up their confidence is vital in strengthening the women's association. It is also important to create a mechanism that would enable the executive member of the women's association to participate in the peasant association's general assembly and executive member meetings. Their involvement in the decision-making would help to reverse the subservient position of the women's associations.

Social constraints are also a major factor restricting women from being active participants in women's association activities. Early marriage is still prevalent among Christian and Muslim families in rural Ethiopia. Among many Muslim families, not only is polygamy practiced, but the emerging conditions may have added to the incentives to marry more than one wife. The present land ownership structure enables co-wives to register as a head-of-household in a peasant association while the husband already owns land in a neighboring peasant association.

In both Christian and Muslim rural communities, religion still permeates every aspect of social and family life. The 1974 Ethiopian Revolution proclaimed Ethiopia to be a secular state and launched efforts to silence those religious traditions which confine women to domestic activities. While these efforts have been somewhat successful, religious traditions continue to gender-segregate the division of labor. These religious and cultural traditions limit male-female interaction. During the field investigation, for example, it was found that the widows and co-wives who are registered members in a peasant association, rarely participated in the peasant association's general assembly meetings.

The Ethiopian government needs to reorganize its efforts to discourage social and religious customs which repress the status of women and their participation in development. While genuine, the mass media campaign (mainly through radio) is not an effective way of reaching rural families. Even in Arsi, where farmers have a relatively better income than in most regions of Ethiopia, this survey, as well as the 1980 ARDU survey showed that only about 30% of the rural families own a radio.

Based on the evidence gathered by observing two peasant associations during field work, the following hypothesis was constructed: one of the most effective ways of easing social constraints on female participation is to initiate discussion on this topic at the general assembly meetings of both the peasant and the

Based on the evidence gathered by observing two peasant associations during field work, the following hypothesis was constructed: one of the most effective ways of easing social constraints on female participation is to initiate discussion on this topic at the general assembly meetings of both the peasant and the women's associations. But the question arises as to whether peasant associations will be willing to discuss such issues. For instance, Hanna Kebede's study, which systematically followed the progress of women since the Agrarian Reform, revealed that when women challenged the practice of dowry and started to discuss their struggle against sexual oppression, conflict ensued in some families and in the peasant associations. In such cases, peasant association leaders have dissolved the women's association or reduced their activities to the promotion of programs emphasizing women's domestic role. (9)

In principle, extending full membership to rural women in a peasant association is the best way of increasing their participation in decision-making and development programs affecting them and their families. This should be a long-term objective. At present, however, cultural and religious barriers restrict women from effectively participating side by side with men. Consequently, the short-term objective should be to attract more women to be active members, and to establish a similar institutional network, from the village to the national level, like the peasant association, that would encourage the development of the women's association as an autonomous legal unit. Strengthening the women's association is one of the most effective ways of realizing the 1975 Agrarian Reform and of promoting equity, efficiency, and productivity in the peasant household.

Peasant head of household and daughter (above). Extension agent advising peasant woman (below).

III. Service Cooperatives

Peasant associations have played a crucial role in introducing and consolidating the Agrarian Reform in Ethiopia. They are now the most prominent peasant institutions in Ethiopia. Yet, the government sees them as an initial organization of the forces of production which need to be transformed gradually into a collective form. Towards this end, the government issued a proclamation in 1978 to facilitate the formation of service cooperatives. Service cooperatives are intended to unite together peasant associations which are considered to be small and weak, in order to take advantage of the economy of large-scale agriculture, commerce and servicing enterprises.

Theoretically, three to ten peasant associations can set up a service cooperative. But on the average about five peasant associations form a service cooperative. Individual peasants are indirect members of a service cooperative through their peasant association. Each peasant association elects three of its representatives to the general assembly of the service cooperative, the highest legislative organ. The general assembly elects three men to an inspection committee and an average of ten men to the executive committee every two years. The executive committee appoints members of the finance, purchasing, education and social subcommittees.

The activities of service cooperatives vary from region to region in accordance with their relative financial and administrative strength. The objective of the cooperatives, in the short term, is to increase the bargaining power of peasants. In the long term, it is to encourage and promote collective agriculture. Its major function is to provide peasant farmers (through their peasant association) with a marketing outlet for their produce, a retail outlet for consumer goods, and to distribute agricultural inputs and credits. The cooperative is also in charge of the development of infrastructures such as schools, clinics and rural roads. Some service cooperatives offer flour and oil milling, and a grain storage facility. They also mobilize peasants to undertake reforestation and soil conservation projects that are vital to the protection of natural resources.

One of the leading features of service cooperatives is that they act as an intermediary between the government agency and peasants in crop marketing, distribution of consumer goods, and agricultural inputs. Following the Agrarian Reform, two government agencies were established that have had considerable control on the marketing and distribution structure. The first is the Agricultural Marketing Corporation (AMC) which has the authority to set prices and to purchase and sell agricultural products. The second is the Ethiopian Domestic Distribution Corporation (EDDC) which supplies consumer goods to the urban as well as to the peasant sector. At present, the service cooperatives, like the government institutions, lack the capacity to handle these functions adequately. If peasant production is to be stimulated, the relationship between service cooperatives and government agencies must be improved, and the cooperatives themselves must be strengthened to assume some of the tasks of government agencies. These issues will be examined in detail in Chapter 5.

In a few of the surplus grain-producing regions like Arsi, peasant farmers are required to sell a certain quota of their produce to service cooperatives at a fixed price set by the AMC. The service cooperatives have to sell all they have purchased to the government parastatal, the AMC, for a profit of no more than five birr (1 US $ is equal to 2 Ethiopian birr.) This profit margin is set by the AMC to off-set the cost incurred in transportation, storage and handling. Most of the chairmen of the service cooperatives interviewed in Arsi reported that the surplus generated from grain marketing was very marginal.

All service cooperatives have a cooperative shop where members can buy food and manufactured goods such as salt, sugar, cooking oil, soap, shoes, textiles, blankets and stationery. They are the major income-generating activity of most cooperatives. The purchasing sub-committee, in consultation with the executive committee, decides on the items to be bought. One or two purchasers will be sent to the regional redistribution center or to Addis Ababa to buy the goods, which are distributed by another government parastatal known as the Ethiopian Domestic Distribution Corporation. The transportation and *per diem* expenses of the purchasers can be of considerable expense to the society since it may take them weeks before they will be able to find the goods and transport them. The profit margin which covers the *per diem* expenses and the transportation cost is about 10% to 15% of their buying price. Prices of consumer goods at services cooperatives are slightly lower than the price of goods purchased from private traders.

Service cooperatives are increasingly undertaking the distribution of fertilizer, improved seeds, and pesticides to farmers through their peasant associations. The number of such cooperatives, are very few in other regions of Ethiopia, but are numerous in Arsi. ARDU transfers this responsibility to service cooperatives when it appears that they have the manpower and the administrative capacity to handle it.

Findings from Arsi show that one of the most effective ways of increasing agricultural production in a relatively short period of time is by making inputs such as fertilizer, improved seed and pesticides available to peasant farmers. But institutional constraints make the availability of these inputs problematic. If the financial and the managerial capacities of service cooperatives are strengthened, service cooperatives could be more effective and efficient in supplying credit and inputs to the peasant sector. This is well demonstrated in Arsi where 75% of the sampled service cooperatives distribute inputs and handle credit repayments with minor assistance from ARDU extension agents (for details see the section on credit participation in Chapter 6).

The Arsi region has one of the most developed service cooperatives in Ethiopia. These cooperatives mobilize resources for the construction of schools, health facilities, feeder roads, water and soil conservation and reforestation projects. Some also run production enterprises such as dairy farms, brick-making factories and improved seed multiplication farm.

Labor, particularly when it is abundant, could be one of the investable resources to enhance agricultural production. Service cooperatives have the potential to serve as the institution to mobilize labor for the development of the peasant sector. They can eventually assume the responsibilities of government institutions, such as crop marketing, retailing and input distribution.

One of the model service cooperatives that is already undertaking these tasks in Arsi is found in the Etheya area, Chilalo Awraja. It serves 10 peasant associations with a total of 2017 members. It was established in 1975 with an initial capital of 30,000 birr. This money was acquired through the contribution of 3,000 birr from each peasant association. It embarked upon its first income-earning enterprise with cooperative shops. This was not profitable at first since the goods did not meet the needs of the members and were considered to be of inferior quality. Then it made a special effort to purchase goods like blankets, sickles and ploughs that are in demand; farmers had been paying higher prices to obtain these goods from private traders. This service cooperative now makes profit from the cooperative shop since most members find and buy consumer goods from it.

Another major source of income is the 400 ha. service cooperative farm. It was established by pooling 40 ha. of adjacent land from each peasant association. Most of the Etheya region is located in a flat fertile area. And most of the peasant associations in the Etheya area are well suited to large-scale mechanized farming. The cooperative effectively used this advantage by increasing their application of improved inputs and mechanized farming. They now have five tractors and three combiners which are used both for the cooperative farm and for rental to other service and producer cooperatives in the area. Mechanized farming has become profitable for this service cooperative; they have recovered the initial cost of the tractors in three years time. They also use the cooperative farm for improved seed multiplication and oil seed planting, a good source of revenue to be reinvested in the cooperative.

The other income-earning ventures are an oil refinery (where the oil seed is readily obtained from the cooperative farm), fuel distribution, garage services and crop marketing. This service cooperative has steadily increased its income through its varied activities. Its capital budget has increased from 30,000 birr in 1978 to 590,188 birr in 1983; its fertilizer distribution from 200 quintals to 1238 quintals; and its improved seed distribution from 1 quintal to 210 quintals during the same year. Grain marketing is the only enterprise which showed a decline from 9831 quintals purchased in 1978 to 5357 quintals in 1983.

The Etheya service cooperative is a classic example of resource mobilization for development. This area had a serious water problem before 1979. In 1979, the service cooperative contributed 40,000 birr, half of the capital required to install pipes to bring water from the nearby town of Gonde, which is 13 km. away. Members provided the labor for digging the well and installing the pipes while ARDU provided the technical support. There are now water pumps every 3 km. between Gonde and Etheya, five water pumps in the town of Etheya and pipe lines are also extended to some households in Etheya.

Another strong service cooperative is found in Chilalo Awraja, Lemo Wereda, whose emphasis is on artisan training and cottage industry projects. It derives a large portion of its income from brick-making, a still factory (which makes agricultural equipment like ploughs and hoes), furniture shops (which make household items like chairs, tables and boxes) and provides artisan skill training to its members. It also has dairy farm, tractor, and combiner services. As of 1983 it had a capital budget of 542,523 birr. It has provided credit to weak service cooperatives in the area that had difficulty obtaining loans from the Agricultural and Industrial Development Bank.

The weakest service cooperatives in Arsi are often found in the low-cereal producing areas which depend largely on livestock and its by-products. A good example is one located 20 km. from the strongest service cooperative in Etheya. It serves three peasant associations in the lowland zone between Dhera and Etheya. The only service it provides is a cooperative shop. Fertilizer distribution is done by ARDU because the cooperative does not have the administrative capacity to handle it. Most farmers in this area depend on livestock and do not have that much surplus grain to sell. Hence, it is not involved in grain marketing. The cooperative shop, its only source of revenue, is well appreciated by members who previously had to walk 10 to 20 km. to obtain some of the basic household goods from private traders. Its capital budget has increased from 6,447 birr in 1978 to 15,565 birr in 1983 mainly from the cooperative shop income.

Having examined the service cooperatives that are considered to be the strongest by the government standard in the northern Shewa region, it is clear that those in Arsi are highly developed and well managed. For instance, one of the strongest service cooperatives in the Deber Sina area (Sife Berte) has one tractor and two mills which are major sources of generating income. It serves three peasant associations and has a capital budget of 109,721 birr. Similar to what was observed in the strong service cooperative in Etheya, the chairman of this service cooperative also reported that grain marketing is their least profitable enterprise. This largely has to do with the operation of the marketing arrangement which will be examined in the next chapter.

The above case studies of service cooperatives demonstrate their potential to become an indispensable peasant-led institution in the agrarian transformation

of Ethiopia. It is important, however, to know their weaknesses so that concerted effort can be made to strengthen them. In this regard, this study attempted to assess farmers' perceptions of the services provided by their service
cooperatives in Arsi (See Table 13).

Table 13

Farmers Perceptions of Service Cooperatives

Respondents' Perception of Services	# Interviewed	% of Interviewed
Find Services to be Satisfactory	84	56%
Don't Find Services to be Satisfactory	66	44%
Total	150	100

Most of the sampled farmers in Arsi (56%) are satisfied with their service cooperatives. The respondents perceptions apply to the overall services given by
the service cooperative.

Those who were dissatisfied with the services were asked the reason why;
their answers are summarized in Table 14.

Table 14

Primary Reasons For Farmers' Dissatisfaction With Service Cooperatives

Reasons for Dissatisfaction	# Interviewed	% Interviewed
Shortage of Manufactured Goods	32	49
Unavailability of Consumer Goods on Time	15	23
Unavailability of Agricultural Equipment	8	12
Lack of Quality in Consumer Goods	5	8
Favoritism in Distribution of Goods	3	5
Shortage of Goods that are Food Items	1	1
Unavailability of Goods Appropriate to Seasons	1	1
Prices for Goods are Expensive	1	1
Total	66	100

Table 14 shows that 49% of the respondents cite shortage of manufactured goods, 23% not receiving consumer goods on time, and 8% not receiving consumer goods of high quality as the main reasons for their discontent with their service cooperatives. In other words, the principle source of displeasure for 80% of those dissatisfied with their service cooperatives is that EDDC does not provide them with an adequate and timely supply of manufactured goods.

The farmers' perceptions of their service cooperatives (as shown in Table 13) was cross-tabulated by the farmers' preferred source for buying consumer goods (Table 15).

72

Table 15

Relationship Between Farmers' Perception of Service Cooperatives and Pre-ferred Source for Purchasing Consumer Goods.

Perception of Service Cooperative

| | Source for Purchasing Consumer Goods | |
	Service Cooperative	Private Trader
Satisfied with the Services	68%	32%
Dissatisfied with the Services	23%	77%

Chi Square 28.3 significant at 0.05 level and beyond (1 degree of freedom)

The findings in Table 15 show a statistically significant relationship between farmers who are not satisfied with their service cooperatives and those who like to purchase their consumer goods from private traders. The majority of the farmers who are satisfied with their service cooperatives (68%) also indicated their preference for obtaining their consumer goods from service cooperatives. On the other hand, the majority of those who are dissatisfied with the consumer goods of their service cooperatives (77%) prefer to buy it from private traders. This suggests that private traders have more access to manufactured goods, and goods that are of better quality than do service cooperatives. Consequently, in regard to consumer goods, most farmers consider the goods provided by traders to be better. This is not surprising since EDDC allocates 20% of its total goods to the peasant sector through service cooperatives and 40% to the private sector.

Farmers were also asked if they knew of the kind of development activity undertaken by their service cooperative. Nearly 80% were aware that their service cooperatives were engaged in development activities. The majority of them indicated (70%) that the principal development activity was input distribution, mainly fertilizer. The other activities were running a dairy farm, soil and water conservation, supporting social services (such as building schools, clinics and feeder roads) improved seed multiplication, oil seed refinery, grain mill, tractor services and building grain storage facilities. It seems that there is a relationship between the range of development activities undertaken by a service cooperative and its relative strength. The majority of the farmers who indicated that their service cooperative was involved in several development activities, lived in Etheya and Lemu areas in Chilalo where there are strong service cooperatives.

The weakest service cooperatives are usually found in lowland areas where ARDU is still active in the provision of fertilizer and improved seed. The preliminary field observation indicates that more service cooperatives in Chilalo are involved in undertaking diverse development activities than in Ticho and Arbagugu Awraja, where service cooperatives are mainly responsible for crop marketing. An average service cooperative in Chilalo is engaged in promotion of self-help activities to improve social services and soil and water conservation practices.

Most of the service cooperatives covered in this survey, particularly those in Chilalo, do not appear to have the serious problems reported by many service cooperatives in other regions of Ethiopia, such as lack of financial resources, administrative capacity, simple writing, bookkeeping, and accounting skills and frequent wide-spread corruption among its leaders. (10) This may be attributed to Chilalo's 15 years of experience in integrated rural development, experience which may have influenced the attitudes of people and local organizations. Furthermore, ARDU extension agents spent considerable time assisting them.

To be sure, a great deal needs to be done to strengthen the managerial capacity of service cooperatives in the areas of bookkeeping, accounting, shop-keeping, and credit and saving schemes. The evidence from Arsi indicates that in a relatively short period of time service cooperatives in some cases have surpassed the original government objectives. With the exception of the problems they face in the distribution of consumer goods, service cooperatives are popular institutions that could bring peasant-led and self-sustaining development in Ethiopia. The future role of service cooperatives should be carefully considered, given that most peasant farmers, at present, would prefer to remain smallholders than join collective forms of production.

IV. Producer Cooperatives

The Ethiopian government sees both peasant associations and service cooperatives as transitional institutions in the socialist transformation of peasant agriculture. In 1979, the government issued an elaborate directive for the *stage-by-stage* conversion of peasant associations as well as service cooperatives into producer cooperatives. The decree on the producer cooperative stated that producer cooperatives are the final stage in the collectivization of the means of production in agriculture.

This transformation is to be fulfilled by means of a three-stage institutional metamorphosis. The first stage is *malaba*, where only land is pooled and the members keep oxen, farm implements and about one fifth of their plots as a family farm. The second stage is *Welaba,* where draft animals and implements become the collective property of the cooperative and individual ownership of about one tenth hectare of land is allowed. The third and final stage is *welanda,* where several *welbas* merge to form an average size cooperative of 4,000 ha. and about 2,000 households. At this stage, all means of production are under the cooperative, all smallholders in the peasant association would join, the service cooperative would be a producer service cooperative (like a commune) and the produce would be distributed based on labor contribution. It is also a stage which will utilize large-scale and mechanized agriculture.

The number of producer cooperatives has steadily grown in Arsi from 149 in 1979, to 283 in 1985. Nearly 70% of them are reported to have reached the *welaba* stage, and none so far are at *welanda* stage. Members of producer cooperatives make up 7% of the rural households in Arsi and cultivate 11% of the crop land, a figure substantially higher than the national average. (11)

The 1979 proclamation on producer cooperatives clearly states that peasants should voluntarily join producer cooperatives. Force or coercion is not to be used. Yet, the government policy directs significant human, financial and technical assistance towards inducing the peasant to join the producer cooperatives. ARDU, carrying out the government's policy, assigned high priority to the delivering of fertilizer, improved seed and pesticide distribution and the sale of such items to producer cooperatives at a reduced price. The focus of ARDU's extension and training services is on reaching farmers working collectively and on strengthening the cooperative movement. The great majority of sampled farmers (90%) think that ARDU's program and agents are concentrating on improving conditions for farmers already in producer cooperatives rather than individual farmers in the peasant association. This view was also shared by many ARDU administrators and field-level extension agents interviewed during the field survey.

The minimum number of people who can form a producer cooperative is four. But experienced extension agents argue that there will be no gain from group farming if the number of farmers in a cooperative is less than 30. They assert that cooperatives with few members have usually ended up requiring a great deal of their time and government resources. What would be the ideal membership size in a producer cooperative is in itself a useful research issue to be investigated further.

Those who want to form producer cooperatives either pool their land if the plots are adjacent to one another, or are given land belonging to the peasant association for collective production. In most cases, the most fertile land that is suited for group farming is given to producer cooperatives. This may mean moving individual farmers into other parts of the peasant association if the land they cultivate is needed by the producer cooperative. Once a producer cooperative is established its chairman automatically becomes the chairman of the whole peasant association, even if it means replacing an already elected official. This gives the chairman additional leverage to influence events and has sometimes created tension between members of the producer cooperative and smallholders in a peasant association.

The administrative structure of the producer cooperative is similar to that of the peasant association. The chairman and most members of the executive committee hold the same positions in the peasant association. The only significant difference is that members of a producer cooperative are divided into production teams which are led by the team leader. There about 15 to 30 members in a team. The team leader is responsible for supervising their work and giving points to their daily labor. The points are added up at the end of the year to determine the value of a member's contribution in money or in kind.

The point system is a controversial issue among members and a source of fear and distrust even among those who are not members of producer cooperatives. The point system is based on the following assessments :

1. The number of hours spent working each day;
2. The nature of the task performed (easy vs. difficult task);
3. The quality of work done (how well the job was done).

In practice, only the first criterion is used by most team leaders. This is mainly because team leaders are inexperienced and are at times unaware of the details of the point system. As a result, many considered the point system to be unfair to those who perform a more demanding task. For instance, in one producer cooperative peasants who graze cattle were given the same points as those who were involved in farming.

There are very few producer cooperatives that are well developed and self-sufficient, while the majority of them seem to be weak and rely heavily on government assistance. An example of a weak producer cooperative is found in a hilly peasant association outside of Asella. This peasant association has 137 members and 500 ha. In 1980, thirty farmers joined together to establish a producer cooperative and the peasant association allotted 60 ha. to them. They received a fertile area of land suited for group farming on the flat portion of the peasant association. The association has not attracted new members since its establishment, which is one of the reasons why it is a weak producer cooperative.

Members of this cooperative have no access to modern equipment and are still at the first stage (melba) using their own traditional farming method. There has been no increase in yields, a situation, that keeps them at the level of smallholders. Their total grain yield in the past three years averaged about 800 quintals. The reasons cited for the decline in production were the frequency of bad weather and the weakness of the point system that does not reward adequately those who work hard. This lack of advancement has made some of them disillusioned about the producer cooperative and many have hinted at their intention to leave it. As one skeptical member put it, "They keep telling us yields will increase in large collective farms. But nothing has improved so far." Consequently, negative attitudes towards the producer cooperative have widely circulated in this peasant association and most are clearly not interested in joining it. Even some members stated that they would like to resign their cooperative membership. The only advantage they seem to gain by remaining is that they pay less in taxes and contribution fees.

The initial capital of this producer cooperative was 90 birr, obtained by member contribution of 3 birr. It then got a loan of 1821 birr from the service cooperative to purchase some equipment. It has not been able to pay back this loan since there has not been any surplus generated from its output after the produce is distributed to members.

In 1981/82, members who had the highest points earned 666 birr, the lowest 494, and the average income was 525 birr. Similarly, in 1982/83, it was 628, 525, and 353 birr. It was reported that the average member of the producer cooperative gets about 550 Birr. Most individual farmers who have a pair of oxen in this peasant association make at least 550 birr. In a good harvest they make between 600 to 700 birr. They also have the same degree of access to inputs as producer cooperative members. This may also have contributed to the lack of interest in producer cooperatives shown by individual farmers.

The major obstacle to the development of this particular producer cooperative is, as the chairman himself pointed out, a natural one. Over half of the area in the peasant association lies on steep hillsides. There would be little advantage gained by pooling land that is not suited to large-scale group farming. For instance, it is difficult to use tractors in this area. They are likely to break down easily. Hence, establishing producer cooperatives without an adequate assessment of its feasibility would weaken the cooperative movement and could contribute to the peasants' negative attitude towards them.

One of the most developed producer cooperatives (Hureta Hetosa) is in Chilalo's Hetosa Wereda. The executive members who can read and write have more detailed information about its members and its activities than any of the other producer cooperatives visited. It is in a peasant association with a size of 800 hectares and 292 households. It is situated in fertile flat land very well suited for collective and mechanized farming. It was formed in 1980 with 45 members who pooled their land (113 ha.) and oxen to cultivate collectively. Each member contributed 90 birr and those who were not able to pay right away were to pay it in three years time by deducting each year from their produce.

The membership of the Hureta Hetosa has grown from 45 in 1980 to 160 in 1984. Most of the members were tenants, landless laborers, and dependents before the Agrarian Reform. Only three of them were former owner-cultivators. Nearly 70% of them were between the ages of 20 and 40. And only 4% were above 60 years old. Most of the members were very enthusiastic about their co-operatives and had joined willingly. The chairman and the rest of the executive members of the producer cooperative also hold the same office in the peasant association. They have some formal schooling and are well respected by members.

In five years, this producer cooperative has expanded remarkably in many aspects (See Table 16). This has greatly contributed to the substantial increase in its agricultural output. As a result, it has become self-sufficient in financing its own development activities, and is now classified as one of the few strong producer cooperatives in Arsi.

While Hureta Hetosa is naturally endowed with suitable land for group farming, there are other explanations for its success; from the outset the leadership of the producer cooperative placed emphasis on the advantage to be gained by the members if their draft power and labor were pooled. Only 25 members out of 160 did not have oxen when they joined the producer cooperative. Thus, the major reason for joining producer cooperatives was not to have access to oxen or to receive government assistance as observed in most cases. Some of the results of pooling their oxen, land and labor can be witnessed by referring to Table 16.

Table 16

A Case Study of a Strong Producer Cooperative in Arsi

Improvement of Indicators Contributing to Strength of Producer Cooperatives

Years of Improvement

1980	1981	1982	1983	1984
Number of Members				
45	91	116	131	160
Size of Cultivated Area				
113	214	290	327	400
Size of Grazing Land				
30	55	55	55	55
Trees Planted in Ha.				
-	1	2	3	7
Number of Oxen				
66	129	140	150	180
Number of Tractors				
-	1	2	2	2
Number of Combiners				
-	-	-	-	1
Total Grain Yield in Quintal				
2653	4729	7670	-	-
Gross Income in Birr				
120,425	164,214	266,724	-	-
Total Expenditure in Birr				
58,016	39,776	27,540	-	-
Net Income in Birr				
62,409	124,438	239,184	-	-

The figures in Table 16 were obtained from the headquarters of the producer cooperative. Most of them were drawn on a chart and posted on the wall so that visitors and other members could see them. The members are very proud of their progress and are quick to point it out to visitors. They have records of all their activities and their transactions, a record which most producer cooperatives lack. Initially, they received training from ARDU extension agents in book-keeping and accounting. But now they do these tasks with little assistance from ARDU agents. This is another indicator of the superior administrative and managerial capacity of this particular cooperative. In most cases, ARDU agents admit that most producer cooperatives need their continuous help in this regard.

Members of the Hureta Hetosa producer cooperative are divided into 5 production teams with 32 members. The team leaders were aware of the flaws in the system for recording the amount of time worked, and indicated that they take into account the quality and difficulty of the task performed when giving points. All the points are added up and divided by the total income to determine how much a point is worth. Once the price for a point is fixed, it is multiplied by the total point earned by a member to determine individual income.

When the income distribution of members was assessed, the range between those who earned the highest income and the average income was found to be small, whereas the range between those in high and low brackets was considerable. From 1980 to 1983 those with the highest income earned 1018 birr, 1080 birr, 1893 birr and 1952 birr; the medium income earned was 948 birr, 978 birr, 1580 birr, and 1630 birr; and those with the lowest income earned 880 birr, 777 birr, 1290 birr and 1330 birr. This suggests that the point system in this developed producer cooperative may have captured the qualitative difference in labor contribution. As the 49-year-old chairman of the peasant association, who had only completed the third grade, said, "we believe in rewarding those who work hard. It is the best way to strengthen our cooperative. Our farmers are producing more and we buy more fertilizer and provide more services to them." The average member of this producer cooperative in the last three years has earned 1160 birr. The exact figure for the individual farmer was not obtained since there was no data on their income. But it was said to be between 700 to 800 birr.

Hureta Hetosa has no outstanding debts. Its consistent increase in production has generated surplus which is invested in financing its development activities. While this study was in progress, they were building storage areas, a garage, a literacy school and recreational facilities. Members were busy digging wells to store animal waste products for a bio-gas stove. They were also in the process of purchasing a grain mill, a piece of equipment which is in great demand throughout the community.

Discussions with ARDU cooperative development agents, the executive committee, and participant observation indicate that the strength of this cooperative has to do partly with the member's ability to effectively pool labor and draft power. The leaders did not alienate peasants by imposing upon them an alien view of collectivization as the primary objective of the producer cooperative.

It should be noted that there are very few producer cooperatives, even among those considered to be the strongest, that can claim of such impressive achievements. A large number of producer cooperatives in other regions of Ethiopia are reported to require a great deal of government assistance. Based on a field visit to producer cooperatives in the Shewa region, it would be fair to say that those in Arsi are at a much higher stage of development. For instance, the average incomes of the two strong producer cooperatives in the Deber Sina area were found to be 550 and 565 birr. And their activities are similar to those of the average producer cooperative in Arsi.

Because the foremost debate in Ethiopia concerns the collectivization of agriculture, this section will be devoted to an assessment of peasants' attitudes toward the government's *stage-by-stage* transformation of peasant association into producer cooperative. Peasant farmers were asked whether they would rather remain smallholders using service cooperatives or eventually join producer cooperatives, as the government intends them to do. Their responses are set forth in Table 17.

Table 17

Farmers' Choice Between Individual or Collective Farming

Smallholder Vs. Collective Farming		
	# Interviewed	% of Interviewed
Respondents Who Would Like to be Smallholders Within a Peasant Association	112	75
Respondents Who Would Eventually Like to Join Producer Cooperatives	38	25
Total	150	100%

The above findings emphasize that in spite of ARDU's inducement policy, the majority of the sampled farmers (75%) wish to remain smallholders. The peasants' attitude on this issue may change in the future. Most farmers do not understand the process of the *stage-by-stage* development of producer cooperatives. Their reaction mainly comes from the unfavorable opinions they have heard expressed about collective farming. At present, collective farming is unpopular even in a highly politicized region like Arsi. These findings have major policy implications for the Ethiopian government and for ARDU's objective, namely, to improve peasant production; they will be dealt with in detail in Chapter 7.

Further analysis of Table 17 according to Awraja reveals a statistically significant relationship between the particular Awraja in which the farmer lives, and the farmer's choice of whether to remain a smallholder or join a producer cooperative. Among the respondents who lived in Chilalo, 36% would like to join producer cooperatives, whereas the figure for Ticho and Arbagugu was 12%. Hence, there were three times as many farmers who wanted to join producer cooperatives in Chilalo than in Ticho and Arbagugu. What may have contributed to this wide difference and what lessons can we learn from it?

1. Farmers in Chilalo have been exposed to integrated rural development projects since 1967 (under both CADU and ARDU), whereas the project was only extended to Ticho and Arbagugu Awraja after 1976 under ARDU. The activities of the ARDU's program in both technical and cooperative development have been focused primarily on Chilalo. As a result, farmers are likely to be more receptive to new ideas and innovations in Chilalo.

2. Farmers in Chilalo are more politically conscious than farmers in Ticho and Arbagugu. They were faced with a peculiar circumstance that had a severe impact on their wellbeing under feudal Ethiopia: tenant eviction was prevalent due to the mechanization of agriculture. Before the Reform, when farming became more profitable with the application of inputs made available to large farmers and landlords, land values had increased dramatically. CADU's extension staff have served as a radical force in politicizing tenants, causing them to react against these conditions. There were protests and sporadic peasant uprisings in some parts of Chilalo before the 1975 Agrarian Reform.

3. Chilalo is in closer proximity to major cities like Addis Ababa, Nazerete, and Deber Zeyite than are Ticho and Arbagugu. Ticho and Arbagugu were not easily accessible since they lacked an all-weather road before 1976. The urgent need for land reform was being discussed in urban areas in the early 1970's. Such news could easily reach Chilalo residents and students. In fact, there were protests and sporadic peasant uprisings against landlords in Chilalo just before the 1975 Agrarian Reform.

4. There is more frequent contact between ARDU extension agents and farmers in Chilalo than in Ticho and Arbagugu. This is partly because there are better roads in Chilalo and partly because there are more extension agents in Chilalo, given its high agricultural potential. As will be examined in Chapter 6, there were considerably more farmers in Chilalo who received advice on crop improvement, farmers who invested in their farm, and farmers who use credit to buy inputs than in Ticho or Arbagugu. A large number of these farmers have experienced an increase in their productivity and attribute this

to ARDU. Thus, ARDU agents may be more likely to influence these farmers to see the advantage of collective farming.

One of the policy implications of the above finding is that farmers in Chilalo that have benefited from the application of modern inputs, from the advice of extension agents and ARDU's program, are likely to be more progressive in their views about collective farming than subsistance farmers with limited exposure, as is the case in Ticho and Arbagugu Awrajas. Farmers in Ticho and Arbagugu have very limited contact with extension agents and are more representative of the average farmer in Ethiopia. Hence, projects which are initially targeted to improve peasant farmers' productivity may also gradually contribute to farmers' willingness to try other forms of production, like producer cooperatives, later on.

Farmers were further asked why they would, or would not, like to join producer cooperatives. Their responses are presented in Table 18 and 19.

Table 18

The Primary Reasons for Wanting to Join a Producer Cooperative

Primary Reason for Joining Producer Cooperative	# Interviewed	% Interviewed
Large-Scale Group Farming Will Increase Yields and Income	15	40
Would be Able to Receive Government Assistance	9	24
Shortage of Oxen (Will Have Access to Oxen)	6	15
To Support Government Policy Towards Producer Cooperatives	5	12
Would Get a More Fertile Plot of Land by Joining a Producer Cooperative	1	3
Land Size Too Small	1	3
Too Old to Farm Individually Would Be Able to Get Support From Others in Producer Cooperative	1	3
Total	38	100

The majority of the respondents (40%) cited that their reason for wanting to join a producer cooperative is to increase their yields and income through group farming. This view was even expressed by farmers who wanted to remain smallholders. Why did this view come to be prevalent among smallholders in Arsi?

Field investigation reveals two important reasons:

1. The government objective as stated in the 1979 Producer Cooperatives Directive, is to bring about agrarian socialism by transforming peasant production into a large-scale mechanized farm under collective ownership of the means of production. This policy assumes that small farms are economically inefficient and that economies of scale based on pooling land, manpower, and implements in producer cooperatives will lead to substantial increases in agricultural output. To be sure, there is some truth to this

argument, particularly in light of the serious problem faced by land fragmentation and the diminishing size of the family farm as discussed in Chapter 2. But it is very far from being the truth and nothing but the truth, as it is single-mindedly pursued by the government. This proposition is disseminated by the mass media and is accepted as a truism by everyone, from high-level officials to field-level extension agents. Needless to say, it is a recurring theme one hears in various circles. In the course of this research, it was frequently observed that political cadres and extension agents reiterate the idea in the peasant association or service cooperative general assembly meetings.

However, there are competing views, in the literature about the economics and dis-economics of scale in agriculture. Farm management studies from one of the most thoroughly researched developing country - India - have established an inverse relationship between farm size and productivity. (12) In other words, small farms showed higher yields per acre than large farms. The most recent study, which is based on cross-sectional data from 15 developing countries showed that there is no real advantage in large farms with regard to higher yield and efficiency per hectare. (13) These issues will be investigated in detail in Chapter 7 while discussing strategies of peasant development.

2. ARDU extension is heavily involved in cooperative promotion. It appears that an extension agent feels that he is well regarded by his supervisors and government administrators if he assists in the establishment of more producer cooperatives. "Agitation" is the term used by extension agents when influencing peasants to see the advantages of establishing a producer cooperative. In fact, some ARDU officials have pointed out that this has contributed to the hasty establishment of producer cooperatives even when they were unwarranted.

Receiving government assistance was cited as the second important reason for wanting to join a producer cooperative. This is a reasonable assessment by peasants since all government agencies assign a high priority to assisting producer cooperatives. For instance, they can obtain an interest-free loan from the surplus generated by their service cooperative and pay lower prices for agricultural inputs and sell their produce at a slightly higher price directly to the AMC. Smallholders who are not members can not sell to service cooperatives at the same rate. This is one of the reasons why some farmers would like to join producer cooperatives. An example of such a farmer lives in the surrounding area of Asella, in a hilly peasant association on Chilalo mountain. He is 51 years old and was twice evicted from his land before the Agrarian Reform. He owns 3 ha. of land, which is adequate for his family. His farm is located on a rugged area that requires strenuous labor and is difficult for oxen farming. His son-in-law is a member of a producer cooperative in Lemu Wereda 20 km. away. He told him that they had access to both tractor and combiner services. As a result, this farmer would very much like to see the establishment of producer cooperatives in his peasant association since they would be able to get government assistance to buy tractors and other modern equipment.

The third important reason for joining a producer cooperative is to have access to oxen. Most of these farmers have only one ox and cultivate a relatively smaller land size, ranging from 0.5 to 1.5 ha. They usually borrow an ox from other farmers and in return assist them in ploughing or harvesting. In a producer cooperative, oxen and other farm implements are made available to members who do not have them; a charge for this service is subtracted from their produce at the end of the year.

The respondents who would like to remain smallholders in a peasant association using service cooperatives were asked the reasons why they do not want to join producer cooperatives. Their responses are summarized in Table 19.

Table 19

Main Reason for Choosing Not to Join a Producer Cooperative

Main Reason for Not Joining a Producer Cooperative	# Interviewed	% of Interviewed
Would Like to Possess Their Own Farm	67	60
Fears That Others Would Not Work as Hard Will Take Advantage of Those Who Work Hard	15	13
Land is Not Suitable for Large-Scale Collective Farming	9	8
Income in a Producer Cooperative is Shared on a Point System Once a Year	5	4
Too Old to Earn Enough Points to Make Sufficient Income in a Producer Cooperative	6	5
Have a Large Family and Will Not Earn Enough for Family in a Producer Cooperative	4	4
Does Not Know Much About Producer Cooperatives	3	3
Work Too Demanding in a Producer Cooperative	2	2
Pastoralist - Only Interested in Livestock, Not Farming	1	1
Total	112	100

Table 19 shows that among the sampled farmers who choose not to join producer cooperatives the largest number of the respondents (60%) indicated their primary reason to be that they wanted to own their own farm.

Several previous studies have suggested that the Ethiopian peasant is strongly attached to his land and would prefer to be a small landowner. (14) In fact, the 1975 Agrarian Reform, which was enthusiastically supported by peasants in Arsi, may have strengthened farmers' desire for ownership of their own plots. The reform abolished tenancy, brought lower land taxes, and may have induced a sense of tenural security among former tenants. This seems to be supported by the findings of the present survey, which found that 63% of the sampled farmers feel secure about their land tenure (See Table 5).

The above findings also concur with the findings of the two other field studies conducted since the Agrarian Reform. They too pointed out the preference of the peasant for individual farming. The first study, which was done shortly after the Agrarian Reform in Arsi, found that peasant farmers would like to own their plot instead of being a member of a producer cooperative for three reasons. First, farmers have little faith in the work point system used to distribute proceeds. Second, they consider the output of collective farms to be low. Third, they have to coordinate their farming activities with that of the collective farm, a commitment which is time-consuming. (15)

The second study undertaken in the northern Gojam and southern Shewa regions, underscored the finding that peasants want the fundamental unit of production to be a small family farm. (16)

The respondents who indicated that land was unsuitable for collective farming lived in peasant associations that are in a very hilly area or have rugged terrain or that are affected by flooding and water drainage during the rainy season.

Table 19 also indicated that a number of respondents seem to distrust the point system as a measure of one's labor contribution to allocate income and produce in a producer cooperative. In fact, further investigation of producer cooperatives revealed that the point system is one of the outstanding issues of debate in the general assembly of producer cooperatives. The point system, for the most part, only takes into account the number of hours worked and not the strenuousness of the work performed.

Thus, given the present developmental stage of peasant farmers, their unfavorable attitude towards joining producer cooperatives and the serious shortage of manpower to effectively implement and manage producer cooperatives, it would seem inappropriate to give preeminence to the formation of producer cooperatives as a precondition for socialist transformation. Instead, it would seem more appropriate to strengthen the service cooperatives which could bring immediate benefits to their members (through labor mobilization) as well as provide facilities for the cooperative movement to take root in Ethiopia.

88

Notes

1. "A Proclamation to Provide for the Public Ownership of Rural Lands," *Negarit Gazeta*, 29 April 1975, pp. 96-97.

2. Marina Ottoway, "Land Reform and Peasant Association: A Preliminary Analysis," *Rural Africana,No. 28*, edited by John Harbeson and Paul Brietzke, East Lansing: Michigan, Michigan State University, Fall 1975, pp. 43-48.

3. Dessalegn Rahmato, *Agrarian Reform in Ethiopia*, Uppsala: Sweden, Scandinavian Institute of African Studies, 1984, p. 82.

4. Alula Abate and Tesfaye Teklu, "Land Reform and Peasant Association in Ethiopia: Case Studies from Two Differing Regions," *Northeast African Studies*, 2 , 2, 1980, pp. 15-17.

5. Yeraswork Admassie, Mulugate Abebe, and Markos Ezera, *Ethiopian Highland Reclamation Study: Report on the Sociological Survey and Sociological Consideration on Preparing Development Strategy*, Addis Ababa: Ethiopia, Ministry of Agriculture, Land Use Planning and Regulatory Department, December, 1983.

6. Dessalegn Rahmato, *Agrarian Reform in Ethiopia*, Uppsala: Sweden, Scandinavian Institute of African Studies, 1984, pp. 84-90.

7. Hanna Kebede and Dejene Abate, *Agrarian Reconstruction in Ethiopia: Women and Rural Development*, New York: UNDP/FAO Project, 1979, pp. 67-72.

8. *Ibid*, pp. 99-100.

9. Hanna Kebede, *The Integration of Women in Agricultural Reconstruction of Ethiopia*, Nairobi: Kenya, Paper presented to the "Workshop on Women in Agricultural Production in the Third World," 1980.

10. Alula Abate, "Peasant Association and Collective Agriculture in Ethiopia: Promise and Performance," *Journal of African Studies*, Volume, 10, No. 3, Fall 1983, pp. 105-106.

11. *Proposal for SIDA Support to Rural Development in Arsi and Bale 1986/87 - 1987/88*, Stockholm: Sweden, December 1985, p. 233.

12. Parnab K. Bardhan, "Size, Productivity, and Returns to Scale: An Analysis of Farm Level Data in Indian Agriculture," *Journal of Political Economy*, Vol. 81(6), November-December 1973: pp. 1370- 1386. For summaries of other empirical studies on this issue, see:
Jagdish N. Bhagwati and Sukhamoy Chakravarty,"Contributions to Indian Economic Analysis: A Survey," *The American Economic Review*, Vol. LIX, No. 4, Part 2, 1969, pp. 40-43.

13. Giovanni Andrea Cornia, "Farm Size, Land Yields and the Agricultural Production Function: An Analysis of Fifteen Developing Countries," *World Development*, Vol. 13, No. 4, pp. 513-534.

14. Allan Hoben, "Perspective in Land Reform in Ethiopia: The Political Role of the Peasantry," *Rural African*, No. 28, edited by John Harbeson and Paul Brietzke, East Lansing: Michigan, Michigan State University, Fall 1975, pp. 67-68.

15. Aster Akalu, *The Process of Land Nationalization in Ethiopia: Land Nationalization and the Peasants*, Lund: Cluck Gleerup, LXXVI, 1982, p. 156.

16. Alula Abate, "Peasant Association and Collective Agriculture in Ethiopia: Promise and Performance," *Journal of African Studies*, Volume 10, No. 3, Fall 1983, pp. 107.

Chapter 5

The Effect of Leading Government Institutions on Peasant Production

The primary government agencies that have a significant effect on agricultural production are concerned with grain marketing, distribution of consumer goods, and the diffusion of innovations and services to peasant farmers. Following the Agrarian Reform, two powerful government agencies emerged to dominate the present marketing and distribution system: these are the Agricultural Marketing Corporation (AMC) and the Ethiopian Domestic Distribution Corporation (EDDC), respectively. These government agencies have an indirect institutional linkage with peasant households through the service cooperatives. The linkage between service cooperatives and these government agencies is an ambivalent one. On the one hand, the service cooperatives are used to extract surplus from the peasantry, while on the other hand, they are instrumental in extending agricultural inputs, household goods, and services to peasants at the village level more effectively and efficiently. The focus of extension services since the Agrarian Reform has substantially changed in respect to its content and its structure. The emphasis of extension is now on cooperative promotion. There are no individual farm visits conducted by the extension agent. The organizational structure of the extension program does not reach peasant farmers at the village level in a systematic way. Farmers receive advice or assistance in groups through service cooperatives or the peasant association.

The role of the AMC in marketing agricultural products and the EDDC in the distribution of consumer goods, and their institutional linkage with peasant institutions, particularly with service cooperatives, is one of the most fundamental issues of debate between the Ethiopian government and donor agencies. The manner in which the extension services are structured and delivered can significantly influence the stimulation of growth in the peasant sector.

Using Arsi as a case study, this chapter will be concerned with the factors that impede the productivity of peasant farmers in the present marketing, distribution, and extension system. It will also present farmers' perceptions towards these government agencies.

I. The Agricultural Marketing Corporation (AMC)

After the first harvest following the Agrarian Reform, peasant food consumption increased as the peasants were freed from the previous obligation of paying land rent. As a result, there was a significant decline in marketed surplus and a sudden rise in food prices in the urban areas. The black market became profitable and private traders started hoarding grain to obtain higher prices. The government decided to intervene in the distribution of agricultural goods to stabilize the market by establishing the Agricultural Marketing Corporation (AMC), in 1976.

The AMC was an autonomous enterprise under the Ministry of Agriculture until 1979, when it was transferred to the Ministry of Domestic Trade. It was given power to purchase and sell cereals and other crops as well as to distribute agricultural inputs. The goal was to gain increasing state control of the agriculture sector by maintaining the supply to urban centers and the military at stable prices, and to bring the smallholders into the market economy. In its initial two years it played a minor role in grain marketing and the price it payed to farmers varied according to their distance from major urban centers. That is to say, farmers near Addis Ababa were payed more than those living further away from it. Its operations have now dramatically increased: it purchased 1.2 million quintals of grain in 1976/77 and 4.6 million of quintals in 1981/82. (1) This has seriously strained the agency's organizational capacity and has resulted in a very high marketing cost that has to be paid by the urban consumers. The rapid expansion of AMC storage centers, two-thirds of which are inefficient, has led to higher transportation and handling costs. Large quantities of grain have been lost due to poor storage facilities and lack of storage space.

The single most important institutional mechanism that has assisted the AMC to expand its purchasing operation is its link with the service cooperative as indicated in Figure 3.

Figure 3

The Operation of the Agricultural Marketing Corporation

Farm Gate Level	Whole Sale Level	AMC Procurement	AMC Selling Price
PEASANT ASSOCIATION	SERVICE COOPERATIVES	AMC	URBAN DWELLERS
	PRIVATE TRADERS	AMC	
	PRODUCER COOPERATIVES	AMC	
	STATE FARM	AMC	

Individual farmers are required to sell a certain quota of their produce to their service cooperatives at a fixed price (farm-gate price) set by the AMC. Once they meet their quotas, they can sell the rest to private traders. Hence, the AMC does not have a monopoly on grain marketing and it seems unlikely that it will be able to attain such a monopoly in the near future, even if the government wishes it to do so. It has to compete with the private sector, whose operation is not well understood. It usually consists of wholesalers, retailers, and small traders. The private traders pay a slightly higher price (2 to 5 birr more) to farmers than the AMC fixed price paid by the service cooperative. Private traders and service cooperatives handle up to 70% of the marketed grain from the peasant farmers. (2)

The AMC set a different price for purchasing grain at the whole-sale level. Service cooperatives and private traders sell what they buy from the peasant farmers to the AMC with a profit margin of 5 birr. Producer cooperatives get a slightly higher price than service cooperatives. In the price ladder, the state farm obtains the highest price for its produce, approximately 20% higher than service cooperatives receive from the AMC. This is meant to strengthen the role of government institutions. Depending on the region, private traders are required to sell between 50% to 100% of the grain they purchase from the peasant farmers to the AMC. In Arsi they have to sell 50% of the grain they bought to the AMC at a price similar to that of the service cooperative. The AMC distributes the grain to urban dwellers through the Urban Kebelle Association which serves as a retailer to the AMC. Private traders are also restricted from moving the rest of the grain beyond their region's border to sell it in other regions. This has created a large disparity in the price of grain in different regions, a disparity that cannot be adequately explained by the high cost of transportation and handling alone.

For example, in March 1984, while this survey was being conducted, a farmer in Arsi sold a quintal of white wheat for 34 birr to the service cooperative. The service cooperative sold it to the AMC at 39 birr. The AMC selling price to urban dwellers (distributed through the Urban Kebelle Association) in Asella (the capital city of Arsi) was 56 birr. In Nazereth, the major town close to Arsi, the price was 60 to 65 birr and in Addis Ababa it was about 79 birr. The open market price in Addis Ababa was about 82 birr. Similarly, in 1985, the farm-gate price for teff, (which is Ethiopia's staple food) in one of the major producing regions of Gojam was about 65 birr, while its open market price in Addis Ababa ranged from 150 to 200 birr.

Private traders pay a more competitive farm-gate price to farmers, an average of 2 to 5 birr more than service cooperatives. The private traders know the open market price and seem to have a network (black market) for getting it to urban areas in spite of the government's restriction to prohibit the movement of grain across regional boundaries. Most urban dwellers buy grain in the open market since the Urban Kebelle Association cannot meet the demand of the consumers and is usually forced to ration a certain amount per household for a certain period of time.

It is against this background that the author will attempt, in the following section, to assess the farmers' attitudes towards the present marketing arrangements which play a significant part in the government's effort to increase peasant production (Table 20).

Table 20

Farmers' Perception of the Present Marketing Arrangement

Perception of Present Marketing Arrangement	# Interviewed	% of Total Interviewed
Do Not Like the Present Arrangement	90	60
Like the Present Arrangement	60	40
Total	150	100

Table 20 shows that 60% of the sampled farmers do not like the present marketing arrangement. They were asked to offer an explanation for their response. These explanations are summarized in Table 21.

Table 21

Primary Reason for Not Liking the Present Marketing Arrangement

Reason for Not Liking the Present Marketing Arrangement	# Interviewed	% Interviewed
Price Offered for Grain is Low	78	85
Payment for Grain is Not Timely	7	8
AMC Does Not Pick Up Grain from Service Cooperatives Resulting in Grain Loss	5	7
Total	90	100

Table 21 shows that 85% of the respondents do not like the present marketing arrangement because of the low price of grain. Therefore, elaboration of price policy is appropriate.

The system of grain procurement by the AMC in Arsi works as follows: each year the AMC, in collaboration with the Wereda Revolutionary Development Committee, assesses the quotas of grain to be delivered by peasant associations and service cooperatives. In Arsi an average of 150 to 200 quintals of grain are delivered by a peasant association to the service cooperative. The exact amount is based on the agricultural potential of the peasant association. The service cooperatives, in consultation with the leaders of the peasant association, set quotas for the amount of grain individual farmers have to sell to service cooperatives, about 2 quintals of his harvest in Arsi.

The AMC sets the price at the farm-gate, wholesale, and retail level throughout Ethiopia. The farm-gate price, which the AMC pays to peasant farmers, is the lowest on the ladder. For instance, in 1985, right after a bad harvest, the farm-gate price for wheat was reported to be 35 birr/quintal, the AMC buying price from the service cooperative was 55 birr and the wheat price at the Naz-ereth market ranged from 80 to 90 birr. (3) In general, the marketing margin between the farm-gate price and the selling price in major urban areas like Ad-dis Ababa for teff, wheat, barely, sorghum, and maize is reported to range from 87% on up to 200%. (4) This is <u>not a profit</u> made by the AMC. There is a great deal of inefficiency in the system involving storage losses and trans-portation and operating costs.

In this survey, farmers were asked whether they are able to sell their grain freely to private traders after selling their required quota to their service cooper-ative (See Table 22).

Table 22

Ability to Sell Grain Freely After Meeting AMC Quotas

Ability to Sell Grain Freely After Meeting AMC Quotas	# Interviewed	% Interviewed
Able to Sell Grain Freely After Meeting AMC Quotas	97	65
Restricted from Selling Grain to Private Traders Even After Meeting AMC Quotas	53	35
Total	150	100

The majority of the sampled farmers (65%) are able to sell their grain freely, but 35% said they are restricted from selling their grain freely after meeting their AMC quotas. A brief review of national policy and its interpretation at the local level is provided below in order to help explain the restriction placed on these farmers.

In three major producing regions in Ethiopia, the AMC, the major govern-ment agency that buys and sells cereals, purchases 85% of the nation's marketed cereals. These are Arsi, Gojam and Showea regions; they contribute to 29%, 33%, and 23% of the total AMC cereal procurement, respectively. (5) In spite of the AMC's uniform farm-gate prices, retail prices, as well as actual farm-gate prices, have varied greatly in regions where the determination of prices depends upon their proximity to major urban consuming centers. Grain prices near Addis Ababa were higher than in other areas. Therefore, the government introduced administrative controls on the movement of grain. Roadblocks were set up on access routes to major towns, especially those leading to Addis Ababa, to control the movement of private traders transporting grains to sell at a higher price in urban areas. In addition, private traders had to deliver at least 50% of what they purchased from farmers to the AMC at a fixed price. Arsi is one of the regions that stringently enforces this regulation on private traders.

In such an environment, merchants do not purchase as much grain from farmers. This regulation was also interpreted by some local officials and political cadres as instituted in order to discourage farmers from selling to private traders. The restriction on farmers from selling freely in towns or transporting it to major urban centers has three consequences:

1. It lowers grain prices, since farmers have to sell most of the grain to the AMC; they cannot export it to major urban centers outside of Arsi.
2. Black market trade in grain has increased as the difference between the farm-gate price and open market prices in urban areas have widened, causing the black market operation to be even more profitable. At the same time, it reduces the competition in farm-gate prices, lowering farmer incentive for increased production.
3. Since the AMC is not capable of collecting quickly all the grain a service cooperative purchases on its behalf, a considerable amount of grain is lost due to rain and insect infestation. The service cooperatives are also restricted from selling grain in town or exporting it to major urban centers.

The AMC's capacity at present is limited. It does not have the staff, storage, and transportation facilities to handle all the grain it buys in Arsi. Compounding this problem is the severe lack of storage facilities faced by most service cooperatives that act as intermediaries in the buying of the grain for the AMC. Most of the grain bought from farmers lies outside the service cooperative (some without canvas covers) waiting to be picked by the AMC. If AMC trucks do not come to pick up this grain from the service cooperatives before the rainy season begins, which frequently happens, this grain will be lost due to rain and insect infestation.

In sum, these findings from Arsi establish that the present marketing arrangement has an adverse impact on peasant production. The AMC's farm-gate price, when compared to the selling price of the urban dwellers, is too low and does not encourage higher production. In fact, at the price farmers presently receive for their grain, they would not be able to buy fertilizer without subsidization. This is one of the reasons why the present marketing system has led to the decline in the amount of fertilizer application among a considerable number of farmers. The regulation which diminishes the role of private traders and enhances the role of the AMC, even when it does not have the capacity to handle all the marketable grain, has increased black market (parallel) activities. This has resulted in an increase of grain price for urban consumers. Thus, neither the farmers nor the urban consumers seem to benefit from the present marketing arrangement.

II. The Ethiopian Domestic Distribution Corporation (EDDC)

The Ethiopian Domestic Distribution Corporation (EDDC) was established in 1976 to provide consumer goods to the urban areas as well to the peasant sector. The EDDC supplied goods to service cooperatives, which in turn made them available to members of the peasant association. Like the present marketing system, the EDDC operated in direct competition with private traders.

Between 1979 to 1982, the EDDC average sale of consumer goods to the private sector was 39%, to the government institutions 21%, to the peasant sector (through the service cooperatives) 20%, to the handicraft producer cooperatives 11%, and to urban dweller associations 9%. (6) These figures show that the availability of consumer goods to the peasant sector (90% of the population) is extremely low.

This section will include an examination of the primary and preferred sources of farmers' consumer goods (both manufactured and edible). Tables 23 and 24 summarize the farmers' responses to questions on this topic.

Table 23

Source of Most Consumer Goods

Place Where Most Consumer Goods are Purchased		
	# Interviewed	% Interviewed
Service Cooperatives	103	69
Private Traders	47	31
Total	150	100

Among the sampled farmers, 69% purchase their consumer goods from the cooperative shop of the service cooperative. This suggests that in spite of some reported shortages, the service cooperatives are the primary distributor of consumer goods in Arsi. This marks an impressive achievement; peasant farmers who live in remote areas and are poor had extremely limited access to consumer goods before the existence of the cooperative shop. A large number of farmers who reported purchasing their goods from private traders were relatively well-to-do farmers who live closer to a small town or market place. A typical cooperative shop of a service cooperative sells cooking oil, sugar, salt, soap, matches, clothes, blankets, and shoes. The number of consumer goods available at the cooperative shop of a service cooperative is determined by its financial strength, distance from urban centers, and its working capital.

Table 24

Preferred Source of Consumer Goods

Source of Preferred Goods	# Interviewed	% Interviewed
Service Cooperative	72	48
Private Traders	78	52
Total	150	100

Further questioning revealed that those farmers who preferred to buy from service cooperatives rather than from private traders did so because of lower prices at the service cooperative and because the cooperative shop was closer (within walking distance) to their home. Most of those who prefer to purchase goods from private traders (52%) indicated that they find goods that are not available at a service cooperative and goods that are of better quality. For example, a number of farmers remarked that it is difficult to get blankets, sickles, and ploughs at their service cooperatives and those that are available do not last long. As a result, they were willing to pay a higher price for the manufactured goods and agricultural equipment which they said are more desirable and of much better quality than those sold at service cooperatives. This suggests that

EDDC is not distributing better quality goods to service cooperatives. Thus, better institutional linkage between the EDDC and service cooperatives that would insure the availability of good products will provide peasant farmers with the incentive to increase their marketed surplus.

III. Extension Services

Before the Agrarian Reform, the main objective of the agricultural extension under the Ministry of Agriculture's Extension Program Implementation Department (EPID) and the Chilalo Agricultural Development Unit (CADU) in Arsi was the diffusion of tested agricultural inputs and practices. The dissemination strategy was based on a *model farmer* who demonstrated the application of the new inputs to neighboring farmers on a *demonstration plot* that was usually located on a major road or marketplace.

Since the Agrarian Reform, the extension structure does not have a direct linkage with farmers at the village level. There is no individual farm visit conducted by extension agents. Farmers receive group advice from either the cooperative farm of the peasant association or the service or producer cooperative farm. The previous extension system under EPID and CADU was criticized for its emphasis on technological improvement to the exclusion of social development.

In Arsi, CADU's *model farmer* approach was abandoned soon after the Agrarian Reform. A new Extension, Education and Cooperative Department was established under the Arsi Rural Development Unit (ARDU). A distinction was made between social and economic development. The social objective became the creation of a self-reliant cooperative community through collective action rather than simply an increase in individual production. The economic objective became the continuation of the integrated agricultural *package* approach of CADU. The main components of the package approach are the distribution of fertilizer and improved seed through credit.

The new extension department as its name suggests, emphasized its orientation toward cooperative development. Its objectives were:

1. to assist in the consolidation of peasant's, youth's and women's associations;
2. to carry out the development and the consolidation of producers' and service cooperatives;
3. to promote non-formal education with social, political and economic content;
4. to promote self-help schemes;

5. to manage extension trials and farmers' demonstration lots;
6. to advise farmers on crop, livestock and improved implements; and
7. to assist in settlement schemes. (7)

In order to attain these objectives, the department was divided into six District Development Offices (DDO) and 57 Rural Development Centers (RDC). There are four DDO in Chilalo and one each in Ticho and Arbagugu Awraja. The RDC are below the Wereda (sub-district) level and are the lowest administrative structure of extension in Arsi. They are one step lower than the Ministry of Agriculture extension which extends as far as the Wereda level. Yet ARDU's extension structure does not reach the peasant household directly. There are 37 RDC (11 Wereda) in Chilalo; 10 RDC (5 Weredas) in Ticho; and 10 RDC (6 Weredas) in Arbagugu.

In 1984 ARDU had 145 Rural Development Agents (RDA) usually referred to as extension agents. Most of them have completed high school and have received at least 1 year of practical training in ARDU. Three extension agents are usually assigned to each RDC. To facilitate the field operation six task forces were created at the headquarters and at each DDO level. Each task force consists of individuals trained in the following fields: agronomy, farm management, plant and animal husbandry, home economics and cooperative promotion.

Rural Development agents are multi-purpose extension agents who disseminate advice on the technical components of the project and perform the task of cooperative development. The rural development agents work with service cooperatives and peasant associations to coordinate self-help schemes and to promote cooperatives. This strategy involves working with selected group farmers from each peasant association. These farmers are known as a production group. The rural development agents also work with women's and youth associations of peasant associations - particularly on the improvement of literacy and the growth of political awareness. At the district level, the rural development agents work closely with the District Revolutionary and Development Committee to integrate local plans into the district and regional development plans.

Because of the wide responsibilities of the rural development agents, ranging from the diffusion of improved inputs and practices to political education and regional planning, there has been very limited achievement in the dissemination of agricultural innovations among small farmers, with the exception of fertilizer, since 1975. The extension agents do not invest enough time in assisting farmers with agricultural problems. This may be the reason why a considerable number of farmers indicated crop losses due to pests, weeds, and flooding.

There is no specific extension department under the Ministry of Agriculture that serves other regions in Ethiopia. Each of the specialized departments of the Ministry of Agriculture (water and soil conservation, livestock, plant husbandry, agronomy, and cooperative development) run their own services down to the sub-district level. Hence, there is no single line of administrative responsibility. The number of extension agents assigned at the district level varies from zero to four depending on the agricultural production of the district.

The findings from Arsi indicate that even ARDU, which has by far a better extension system than that in any other region under the Ministry of Agriculture, is prevented from effectively reaching peasant farmers because of the following reasons:

1. The organizational structure of the extension does not reach the village level in a systematic way.
2. The excessive variety of responsibilities of the extension agents has drastically reduced the attention paid to the dissemination of information about agricultural innovation.
3. The lack of a fixed schedule of visits from extension agents to selected farmers from the peasant association weakens the link between extension agents and farmers.
4. There is no single organizational structure for technical support to the extension staff.
5. There is no coverage and regular contact between extension agents and farmers.
6. There is no structure to generate information from farmers and extension agents for use in a research design.
7. There is no coordinated linkage between farmers, the extension service and the research department.
8. There is an absence of an adequate number of well-trained and experienced extension agents (particularly subject matter specialists) to serve as a referral and support system.
9. There are no transportation or housing facilities for extension agents.

The above problems are not peculiar to the ARDU extension. They are, in fact, more prevalent in extension programs in other regions of Ethiopia. A concerted effort should be made to address these problems if the extension program is going to be effective in attempting to increase peasant productivity.

Farmers were asked to identify the most serious problems they face in farming and whether ARDU's extension program was effective in dealing with it. It was found that a shortage of oxen, decreasing size of landholding, flooding as the result of poor land drainage, uncertainty of rainfall, a shortage of improved seed, post-harvest losses due to pests, too many weeds and delay in the delivery of fertilizer were all serious problems encountered by farmers. These problem will be discussed below in the order of their importance.

Oxen are the most important animals in Ethiopian agriculture, and are used for both ploughing and treshing. The largest number of the sampled farmers indicated that a shortage of oxen is the most serious problem they face in farming operations. A large number of the farmers use the same oxen for both plough-ing and harvesting. These farmers added that their oxen become very tired dur-ing the long dry season when forage is not as readily available as usual and when treshing is done by ox-trampling. Given that a number of farmers also are experiencing shortages of land for grazing and over-crowding, it is inevitable that the longevity and health of oxen will be affected.

The 1980 ARDU survey also indicated that 59% of the sampled farmers had either one or no oxen. (8) This suggests a shortage of oxen since a pair of oxen is needed for ploughing. The availability of oxen is an important factor in the expansion of cultivatable land, particularly since a shortage of cultivatable land is the most serious problem faced by the second largest number of respondents.

The second largest number of respondents complained that they possess too small of a landholding. They live in highland and medium altitude zones which are relatively fertile but densely populated. A number of respondents indicating land pressure and parcelization as serious problems also lived in these zones. This tends to give further support to the findings reported in Table 10 and 11 in Chapter 4, which show the statistical relationship between ARDU ecological zones and size as well as membership in a peasant association.

The third largest number of respondents cited flooding as their most serious problem in farming. Farmers in Arsi experience two kinds of flooding prob-lems, depending on the terrain and the slope of the area: the first kind is experi-enced in the highland or the medium altitude zone, where the land is relatively flat. In such cases, the water does not drain well during the rain season and stays on the crop land for a long time, disrupting the normal growth and gesta-tion period. Most farmers who experienced this kind of flooding live in Sagure, Bekoji, Koffele RDCs in Chilalo, and Robe RDC in Ticho. The second type of flooding is frequently found in peasant associations that are in a hilly area and have steep slopes. In such cases fast-flowing water washes away fertilizer , planted seeds, and soils.

The fourth largest number of respondents cited two different sets of prob-lems. One is an obligation to participate in various activities in the peasant as-sociation that usurp time normally used to tend their farms, particularly during the planting season. The two frequently cited activities were farming for the collective farm of a peasant association or service cooperative and farming for other families in the peasant association whose head of household is serving in the military.

The fifth largest group of farmers indicated weeds to be a serious problem. ARDU also reports that about 25% of the crop losses in Arsi are due to weeds. (9) The vast majority of the sampled farmers did not use herbicides. Moreover, the traditional methods of seed preparation, intensity of cultivation, and broadcasting are factors contributing to weed control. This could be addressed by relevant lessons on improved cultural practices conducted by ARDU agents.

ARDU's plant husbandry department has conducted herbicide trials for wheat, barley, and maize and has made several recommendations. But what seems to be lacking is the dissemination of these herbicides to farmers and the gathering of feedback about their effectiveness for the research department. It is this aspect of the role of the extension program in Arsi and in other regions of Ethiopia that is lacking.

Farmers were also asked to indicate the second most serious problem they faced in farming. The four most serious problems reported by the majority of farmers in order of importance were shortage of improved seed, post-harvest losses due to pests, delay in the delivery of fertilizer and shortage of agricultural equipment.

The largest number of the sampled farmers (15%) reported that the second most serious problem they face in their farming operation is shortage of improved seed. This seems to be supported by the findings of this survey where only 2% of the sampled farmers reported buying improved seed. The availability of improved seed to the peasant sector in Ethiopia is extremely limited. It is estimated that of the total 26,500 tons of improved seed the country produces each year, well over 18,000 tons (70%) are distributed mainly to state farms, and some to settlement programs. Only 4000 tons were distributed to the peasant sector, of which ARDU receives 2000 tons (7%). (10) In addition, due to the presence of ARDU, Arsi is the only region in Ethiopia which develops, multiplies, and distributes its own improved seed. This suggests that a large number of the sampled farmers do not have access to it. This may be because improved seed is made available to state farms and producer cooperatives first.

The farmers affected by post-harvest losses due to pests, specifically rats and grain fungi, were mostly found in the medium altitude and lowland zones. A number of them reported that the pesticide given by ARDU extension was not effective.

Two reasons were found for the delay in the delivery of fertilizer: (1) The delay is caused by the AMC's "inefficient delivery" to the service cooperatives; (2) the delay is a result of "witheld delivery" because of lack of repayment of credit. Peasant associations take the responsibility for credit collections and, in some cases, fertilizer delivery has been delayed because some members have not paid their debts from the previous year.

All the respondents who indicated lack of agricultural equipment to be their most serious problem have reported their dissatisfaction with the services given by their service cooperative. Most of them have indicated lack of agricultural equipment to be the major reason for their dissatisfaction. The equipment most farmers use are ploughs, sickles, hoes, spades and pitchforks. These are essential in farming and the shortage is likely to affect peasant production.

A. *Extension Effectiveness in Addressing the Problems of Farmers*

The majority of the sampled farmers (79%) believe that the extension services do not adequately respond to the kinds of problems they face in their farming operations. What might be the possible reason for this belief?

It should be noted that farmers were asked to present the most serious problems, as they see them. As a result, a number of the economic, political, and environmental problems they have identified may not even be seen as problems by ARDU agents. Secondly, the most serious problems faced by farmers -- the shortage of oxen, too small farm, flooding, too many activities in their peasant association -- are difficult for an extension agent to contend with.

But a large number of the respondents face problems which can be ameliorated by the ARDU extension program. These include the shortage of improved seed, post-harvest losses due to pests, too many weeds and shortage of agricultural equipment. Most of the respondents who indicated a shortage of improved seed as a major problem have never used improved seed, but they have heard about its usefulness. All of these respondents use fertilizer only. A very small number of sampled farmers are using improved seed along with fertilizer.

Most respondents with post-harvest loss problems reported that they had not received ARDU's advice on post-harvest loss, and those who have received advice reported that the insecticides they use are not effective.

The farmers indicating too many weeds as a problem lived in relatively fertile peasant associations. The weed problem could be controlled through improved farming practices, provided that the relevant messages are transmitted by extension agents.

It seems that a number of the problems farmers face could be addressed by the ARDU extension program, if there were a balance between the extension agents' allocation of time for technical agriculture and for cooperative development. The emphasis of the extension program has increasingly been on cooperative development. The lack of a feedback mechanism between farmers, extension agents and researchers compounds the above problems farmers face. For example, ARDU's plant husbandry department has conducted numerous herbicide trials and made recommendations. (11) But very few farmers are using herbicides.

These findings suggests that ARDU's extension program is not at present fully answering peasant farmers' needs. These problems are most likely to affect the extension programs in other regions of Ethiopia which have a much lower ratio of farmers to extension agents, and extremely limited research facilities as compared to those in Arsi.

B. Extension Services for Women

Project managers deliver resources and services to women through one of three possible approaches:

1. projects targeted to women only;
2. women as components of larger projects; or
3. fully integrated projects. (12)

Each choice made between the above approaches involves serious trade-offs. Projects that are targeted to women are most likely to serve the recipients' needs. Women staff members and beneficiaries feel free to participate in the decision-making process without male domination. At present, however, there are too few trained female personnel in Ethiopia for women-specific projects to be successful.

The second approach, fully integrated projects, allows for an equal flow of resources to both men and women, without a special program for women. Unfortunately, evidence to date from a cross-sectional data indicates that resources rarely reach women. The integrated approach makes women who lack access to land, wealth, credit, political power, time, education, and organization, dependent upon their husbands for these resources. (13) Another study also showed that while the men benefit from credit, technology, and training, women's income-earning potential is marginalized because the type of activities in which they are engaged are not capital intensive, and benefit less from the modern devices. (14)

The third option is to implement a program which views women's issues as an integrated component of a larger project. Project histories indicate that this approach tends to emphasize the women's domestic role and underestimates her contribution to agriculture. In theory, the women's unit could benefit from its ability to draw upon the resources of the larger projects. In most cases, however, the women's component suffers in competition for project resources and lacks sufficiently trained personnel with the appropriate administrative skills. The Home Economics unit of the Ministry of Agriculture illustrates well the inadequacies of this structural method.

The Home Economics unit, the principal means of reaching rural women in Ethiopia suffers from the narrow emphasis of the *home-maker* role in its curriculum and its limited resources and staff. In Arsi, as well as in other regions of Ethiopia, the emphasis on the use of the Home Economics program to reach women has created a dual system - agricultural extension for men and Home Economics for women.

In principle, ARDU's extension programs at the District and Rural Development Centers should provide the full gamut of project components rather than rely on the limited Home Economics program. Women are supposed to receive training in agriculture, income-generating enterprises, and organizational management and budgeting. In practice, only men participate in the District and Rural Development Centers' farmers training courses. In addition, the program also suffers from an insufficient number of female extension agents. Of the 145 extension agents only 10 were women.

In this survey, the sampled farmers were asked if they are aware of ARDU's extension services reaching women in their peasant association. About half of them responded in the affirmative. This is a significant improvement, given that extension programs for women prior to the Agrarian Reform were extremely limited. The establishment of women's associations has greatly facilitated the work of the extension service in reaching women. But the majority of these respondents (75%) stated that the courses offered concentrated on literacy, child care and home improvement. While these skills are important, the program neglects women's crucial role outside the home. These findings echo the recurrent theme in women's and developmental literature which emphasize the fact that extension services targeted to women in developing countries fail to provide adequate agricultural training. (15) In some of the cases when women received agricultural instruction, further examination revealed that it was largely limited to vegetable gardening and nutrition.

Women's contribution to agriculture has been grossly under-represented. This is because of the absence of reliable information on the tasks performed by rural women. A mechanism for generating data on rural women is vital to project planning and implementation. The establishment of women's associations could greatly facilitate data collection but extension services have not yet utilized this potential. Extension agents should work with women's associations to produce a *gender-allocation study* of the agricultural and the household activities that occupy women's time. This would assist in the design of labor-saving devices or innovations that would enable women to participate in income-generating activities. For example, since ARDU's water supplies are located in small towns, women have to travel long distances to get water. If ARDU's strategy changes to a village-based water system, women will need to walk less and will have more time for other activities. Identifying women's activities and work patterns would help the extension service to coordinate its efforts to involve women in a project. In addition, such information would provide the necessary basis for identification, dissemination and adoption of innovations by women. It would also make the extension program more relevant to women.

The three extension approaches (discussed earlier) in reaching women have their relative strengths and weaknesses. The challenge confronting the extension program in Ethiopia, including the one in Arsi, is to adapt the most innovative aspects of each approach and to restructure the Home Economics program so that a greater number of women can be reached through the extension services.

108

Notes

1. *Ethiopia: Review of Farmers' Incentives and Agricultural Marketing and Distribution Efficiency*, Washington D.C.: The World Bank, March 1983, p. 44

2. *Ethiopia: The Agriculture Sector - An Interim Report*, Washington D.C.: The World Bank, 1983, pp. 23-27.

3. *Review of the Arsi Rural Development Unit*, Stockholm: Sweden, SIDA, p. 8.

4. *Ethiopia: The Agriculture Sector - An Interim Report*, Washington D.C.: The World Bank, 1983, pp. 26-27.

5. *Ethiopia: Input Supply, Credit, and Cooperative Development*, Wahington D.C: The World Bank, 1984, PP. 12-15.

6. *Ethiopia: Review of Farmers' Incentives and Agricultural Marketing and Distribution Efficiency*, Washington D.C.: The World Bank, March 1983,*IBID*, p. 50.

7. *ARDU, Annual Report*, 1981/82, Asella, Ethiopia, publication No. 22, 1981, p.11.

8. *Investigation on the Impact of the Agrarian Reform on Peasants' Income and Expenditure Patterns, 1980.* Asella: ARDU Publication No. 18, October 1981, p. 94.

9. Beteru Haile, *On The Activities of the Plant Husbandry Department.* ARDU Publication No. 24, Asella, 1983, p. 48.

10. *Ethiopia: Review of Farmers' Incentives and Agricultural Marketing and Distribution Efficiency*, Washington D.C.: The World Bank, March 1983, p. 23.

11. Beteru Haile, *On The Activities of the Plant Husbandry Department*, ARDU Publication No. 24, Asella, 1983, pp. 49-52.

12. Kathleen Cloud, *Gender Issues in AID's Agricultural Projects: How Efficient Are We?* Washington D.C.: United States Agency For International Development, Office of Evaluation, May, 1985.

13. Marguerite Berger, Virginia Delancey, and Amy Mellencamp, *Bridging the Gender Gap in Agricultural Extension*, Washington D.C.: International Center for Research on Women, 1984.

14. Kathleen Cloud, *Gender Issues in AID's Agricultural Projects: How Efficient Are We?* Washington D.C.: United States Agency For International Development, Office of Evaluation, May, 1985.

15. Eleen M. Charlton, *Women in the Third World Development*, Boulder: West View Press, 1984, pp. 59-101. Also see:

Irene Tinker and Michele Bo Brasmen, *Women and World Development*, Washington, D.C.: Overseas Development Council, 1976.

Chapter 6

Peasant Perceptions of the Impact of Integrated Rural Development Programs in Arsi

A. Change in Agricultural Production of Household

For the purpose of this survey, agricultural production is defined as the total output in quantity per household. The *total output* consists of the crops of primary importance in Arsi. These are wheat, barley, teff, sorghum and maize.

The most significant contribution of the integrated rural development of programs (CADU/ARDU) to agricultural production is the *package* program which includes the dissemination of high-yielding varieties of wheat and barley on credit. As a result, of this program the yield of the two dominant crops - wheat and barley - has increased on the average from 5.8 qts/ha. in 1966 to 20 qts/ha. in 1980 for wheat, and from 10 qts/ha to 17 qts/ha. for barley. (1)

Farmers were asked if their agricultural production has increased since the Agrarian Reform (See Table 25). Agricultural production has increased among 48% of the sampled farmers and decreased among 39% since 1975. The principle goal of the interview process was to provide an idea of whether or not there was a change in the rate of agricultural production, specifically in those crops the farmers consider to be important.

Table 25

Change in Agricultural Production Since 1975

Change in Agricultural Production	# Interviewed	% Interviewed
Production has Increased	72	48
Production has Decreased	58	39
Same as Before	20	13
Total	150	100

These findings, which report that the majority of the farmers experienced an increase in agricultural production, correspond with the two other studies undertaken after 1975. The first one reported that total grain production in the peasant sector was 6.5 million quintals in 1980. (2) Although there is no baseline figure for total production prior to 1974 to provide a meaningful comparison, it is unlikely that it exceeded 5 million quintals. The second finding showed an increase in the average annual consumption of wheat from 41 to 85 kgs. since 1975, which indicates an increase in agricultural production as well. (3)

To identify factors which may have induced an increase or decrease in the *output per rural household*, the findings of Table 25 were cross-tabulated by: (a) Awrajas, (b) crops considered to be of primary importance, (c) farmers' status before 1975, (d) size of cultivated area, (e) age of the household, (f) literacy, (g) major occupation of the head on the household, (h) land fragmentation, (i) land security, (j) farm investment, (k) family income, (l) fertilizer consumption, and (m) marketing arrangement. The only significant statistical relationship revealed by the cross-tabulation was between the size of cultivated area and family income.

Although there was no significant relationship between Awraja and agricultural production, a useful insight was gained when examining the respondents who reported increase production. Sixty-three percent of these farmers live in Chilalo, twenty-two percent in Ticho and fifteen percent in Arbagugu. On further examination, it turned out that a large number of the respondents were from areas ecologically well-adapted for wheat and barley cultivation. This suggests that increases in agricultural production occurred among more farmers who consider wheat and barley to be their primary crops. Given that improved varieties of wheat and barley were first introduced in Chilalo, it is logical that considerably more farmers in Chilalo reported an increase in agricultural production.

The majority of those farmers who reported an increase in agricultural production were those who profited from an increase in cultivatable land combined with an increased application of fertilizer, as opposed to those farmers with only an increase in either cultivated area or fertilizer use.

An investigation of the respondents whose agricultural production has decreased in spite of a large cultivated area (3.01 to 8 ha.) revealed the importance of agro-climatic conditions. The majority of these farmers lived in the highland areas of Sagure and Bekoji RDCs where flooding is a serious threat, and in the lowland Dhera RDC where uncertainty of rainfall is a major problem often faced by farmers.

To illustrate the adverse effect of too much or too little rainfall, the responses of two farmers are summarized below. The first farmer lives in the highland area of Chilalo (Segure RDC) in a PA with 1000 ha. and 249 members. He has 10 children and was a tenant and owner-cultivator before 1975. His total landholdings are 4.5 ha., of which he cultivates 3.5 ha., and leaves the rest for grazing. He does not use fertilizer, since a large portion of it was washed away by rainfall about three years ago. He indicated that he had received advice on soil conservation from ARDU agents at the service cooperative. But he added that it was not effective in dealing with flooding.

Another farmer in the lowland zone of Chilalo (Dhera RDC) with a cultivated area of 4.0 ha., reported a decrease in his output. Maize is his primary crop. It is planted during the short rainy season between February and March (known as "belg"). The "belg" period has been unpredictable and there has not been adequate rain for planting maize for the past two years. He cited this as a major reason for the decrease in productivity over this period.

A closer examination of those who reported an increase in agricultural production and in their level of fertilizer consumption revealed that farmers with cultivated areas between 1.01 and 2 ha. comprised the majority of this group (45%); the minortiy were farmers that possess more than two 2 ha. Given that farmers with 1.01 to 2 ha. are the largest group with increased productivity and increased fertilizer use, it is plausible to argue that fertilizer application contributes more significantly to increases in agricultural production than does farm size.

There was a statistically significant relationship between farmers who reported a change in agricultural production and a change in the size of cultivated area following the Agrarian Reform: 65% of those with increased production also indicated an increase in cultivated area. An investigation of the 65% of those with increased cultivated area and greater agricultural production showed that two-thirds of these respondents were former tenants as opposed to one-third who were former cultivators.

One of the former tenants interviewed lives in Asella RDC, in a peasant association with 800 ha. and 179 members. He is 60 years old and has 7 children. His total landholding is 3 ha., of which he cultivates 1.5 ha. His primary crops are wheat and barley. He received an improved variety of wheat from ARDU which has markedly improved his output. He was a former tenant and was evicted from his land twice before the Agrarian Reform. He now feels secure about his land tenure. He is a regular credit participant and has been using 50kg. of fertilizer consistently since 1975. He indicated an improvement in his agricultural production and income since the Agrarian Reform. He believes that ARDU has contributed to his increased agricultural production through its provision of fertilizer and improved seed.

Among the respondents who reported a decrease in size of cultivated area as well as agricultural production, two distinct groups were identified. The first is a group of former owner-cultivators who used to own between 7 to 15 ha. before the Agrarian Reform. The second group is made up of former tenants who used to cultivate considerably more land prior to 1975 than at present. A good representative of the second group is the man in Dikiss RDC, Ticho Awraja. He lives in a peasant association of 880 ha. and 280 members. He owns 2 ha. of land and he cultivates all of it. Although a former tenant, he cultivated about 10 ha. of land prior to 1975 under a tenancy arrangement sharing one-third of his total harvest with his former landlord. He attributed the decline in his agricultural output to a decrease in his cultivatable area.

Table 26

Relationship Between Change in the Amount of agricultural Production and Family Income

	Change in Family Income			
	No Change	Has Increased	Has Decreased	# of Cases
Change in Production				
Same as Before	35%	15%	50%	20
Has Increased	14%	72%	14%	72
Has Decreased	19%	14%	67%	58

Chi Square 57.7 Significant at 0.05 level and beyond (4 degrees of freedom)

Two distinct groups of farmers emerged when the 72% of the respondents with increased agricultural production and income were examined. One group were former tenants (64%), a large number of which indicated an increase in agricultural production. The second group are farmers who cultivate a relatively smaller area of 0.50 to 2 ha. but who are regular credit participants. They purchase fertilizer using credit, and report an increased application of fertilizer since 1975. The findings above add to the development literature which asserts that an increase in agricultural production is most likely to result in an increase in family income and vice a versa.

B. Crop and Livestock Improvement

1. Crop Improvement

The majority of the sampled farmers (77%) indicated that they have received advice/assistance on crop improvement. This advice/assistance included the dissemination of fertilizer and improved seed and the introduction of improved husbandry practices such as seed bed and soil preparation, proper seeding rates, and pest control.

The majority of the respondents (80%) who received advice on crop improvement were from Chilalo, 70% from Ticho and 60% from Arbagugu. The fact that the smallest number of the respondents receiving advice on crops are in Arbagugu may be attributed to two factors: first, most of the crop research stations are in Chilalo, which is well suited for crop cultivation, as opposed to Arbagugu, which is in the lowland. Second, Further analysis revealed that most of the respondents who have not received advice on crops are farmers who have never used fertilizer or credit to buy inputs. This suggests that receiving advice on crop improvement is likely to result in the use of credit.

The advice farmers received on crop improvement was considered to be helpful by the vast number of farmers throughout Arsi.

2. Livestock Improvement

The livestock program includes breeding, preventive and curative services. The breeding program focuses on dairy improvement by upgrading dairy cattle by cross-breeding selected local cows with foreign breeds. But this practice has been limited to a few service cooperatives since the Agrarian Reform and is not extended to individual farmers. There is little effort to make oxen more accessible, an improvement which could significantly aid many farmers who report a shortage of oxen.

Preventive veterinary service, specifically vaccination is the most common service reported by a large number of the respondents. It is reported that out of the total herd population of 1.6 million animals an average of 1 million animals per year have been vaccinated since 1976. Over 80% of these farmers have reported this service to be useful. (4)

C. Forestry, Soil Conservation, and On-Farm Grain Storage

1. Soil Conservation

The advice provided by extension agents is centered on maintaining good farm management and preventing soil erosion by the building of terraces to alter the steepness of the slope. Advice on good farm management included the following:

(1) leave crop residue on the ground to increase the rate of infiltration and the amount of water stored in the ground;

(2) plough and plant along the contour and not up and down the slope; and

(3) practice crop rotation. Avoid cultivating the same crop each year.

Among the sampled farmers, 58% reported having problems with soil erosion. In light of the distinctive ecological variations between the three Awrajas, the findings above were cross-tabulated by Awraja to see if there is a relationship between the Awraja a farmer lives in and problems with soil erosion. The results showed a statistical relationship between the Awraja in which a respondent lives and problems with soil erosion. Sixty percent of those who experienced soil erosion problems lived in Chilalo Awraja, 36% in Ticho and 13% in Arbagugu Awraja. In both Chilalo and Ticho, a large number of the respondents who have problems with soil erosion live in the highland areas. These areas receive heavy rainfall during the big rainy season (1,000-1500) and have heavy clay and acidic soil, which does not drain water well. In Arbagugu most areas are in the lowland with an average annual rainfall of 600mm. Thus, it is reasonable to expect that the incidence of farmers suffering from problems with soil erosion would be considerably lower in Arbagugu than in Chilalo.

The majority of the respondents in all Awrajas attributed soil erosion to heavy rainfall. The most frequently witnessed form was rill erosion, which is caused by water flowing from the hills to the farm areas. An important question for future research is whether land exploitation patterns may have contributed to the problem.

The ARDU extension agents seem to be well aware of this problem. The majority of the farmers in Chilalo indicated receiving advice on soil conservation and also considered the advice to be helpful. A considerable number of respondents who do not have or do not recognize having problems with soil erosion are still receiving advice on the erosion prevention measures. These prevention measures are essential in protecting soil nutrients and reducing soil degradation. The measures will assist in preventing rill erosion from developing into guilles as presently witnessed in the northern highlands of Ethiopia.

The other kind of erosion that was observed in major livestock areas was caused by over-grazing. During the long dry season there is usually little grass and vegetation and the trampling of the cattle on bare ground reduces the soil water preservation capacity. Erosion due to wind or rain could result from over-grazing.

The vast number of farmers (90%) who received advice on soil erosion considered it to be helpful in making them aware of its adverse effects. A useful addition to the extension program on soil erosion program would be to introduce some grazing control measures to peasant associations that are experiencing over-grazing.

2. *Afforestation Activity:*

The services given by ARDU extension agents on afforestation mainly concentrated on two areas:

1. The distribution of seedlings to be planted, and
2. transmission of messages through group meetings in peasant associations or service cooperatives concerning the importance of planting and protecting trees.

The results of this survey showed that 60% of the sampled farmers find fewer trees on and around their farms than 10 years ago. A 1984 publication reported that since 1976/77, 17.4 million forest seedlings have been distributed throughout the Arsi region. (5) In the Arsi region there are approximately 235,378 households. (6) ARDU distributes these seedlings to peasant associations which in turn give them to their members or plant the seedlings with groups in the peasant association. If the 1.7 million seedlings had been distributed in Arsi, there would be about 70 seedlings per farm family and the number of trees on the farm would be unlikely to be fewer now than 10 years ago. Thus either ARDU may not have distributed that many seedlings or the seedlings have an extremely low success rate after planting.

Since one of ARDU's objectives is experimentation with different extension methodologies, and since deforestation is an enormous nation problem facing Ethiopia today, an effective afforestation scheme trial by ARDU will have national significance.

3. *On-Farm Grain Storage:*

Approximately 30% of the grain in the world is sacrificed to post-harvest losses. (7) ARDU's extension efforts to prevent post-harvest losses focused on two areas:

(a) construction of grain storage facilities that were resistant to insects, rodents, and rain. These are to serve as a model for farmers to build their own improved storage.

(b) Distribution of pesticides, especially against rats and insects.

The findings from this survey showed that 40% of the respondents experience a loss of 20% to 30% of their crop. The causes of post-harvest losses included rats, mice, molds, and seeping of water into storage facilities. Most farmers who live in the lowland areas reported rats and insects to be the cause of post-harvest grain losses in the lowland areas. In contrast, grain fungi and high moisture content during the storage were main cause of crop losses in the highland.

Among the sampled farmers who have received and benefited from advice on how to prevent post-harvest losses, the largest number lived in Chilalo. One of the major activities of ARDU is an attempt to reduce grain losses due to poor storage facilities at the Rural Development Center (RDC) level. In the course of the visits conducted by interviewers to randomly selected centers most of the model storage facilities constructed by ARDU were found in Chilalo. There was one in both Ticho and Arbagugu. Hence, it is reasonable to expect that a large number of farmers have benefited from the demonstrations of improved grain storage. Among the respondents who indicated that the advice from ARDU was not helpful, nearly all said the pesticides they have used against rats have not been effective.

Some of the model storage facilities constructed at Rural Development Centers do not serve as good examples. These storage facilities have vertical supports which are too close to the ground; they should be at least half a meter above the ground. There were also storage facilities that did not have a tin cover on the top of each vertical support to prevent rats from climbing up into the stored grain.

As recorded in the previous chapter, ARDU's extension agents do a poor job of transmitting a consistent and systematic message to the peasants. ARDU extension presently focuses on the distribution of pesticides against rodents and insects to prevent grain loss in storage. These efforts are helpful, but do not adequately prepare farmers to deal with grain loss problems at the early stages by demonstrating the appropriate technology and preventative techniques that could be easily understood and easily available to the farmer. Emphasis should be placed upon demonstrating better methods of harvesting, drying and storing, as well as methods of preventing damage by insects, rodents, and molds, and controlling moisture content and temperature ahead of time. These measures will improve that quality and the nutritional value of the grain in storage.

D. Family Income

The Ethiopian Government has made a concerted effort to use the Agrarian Reform to improve the welfare of peasants relative to urban dwellers. In this section farmers' perception of whether their incomes and social services have improved following the Agrarian Reform will be presented.

Pre-tests of the questionnaire revealed that farmers are unlikely to give reliable information on sensitive issues like yields, income, and savings. This is because they fear taxes or requests for self-help contributions. Thus, the question posed regarding change in family income did not involve a specific figure. Besides, the objective of this study is to offer farmers' general views on income improvement following the Agrarian Reform.

The findings showed that family income has increased for a slight majority of farmers (42%) in the sample group, decreased for 39%, and has remained unchanged among 19% of the sampled farmers. Through an examination of the respondents with increased income the following characteristics emerged:

1. 68% live in Chilalo, 24% in Ticho, and 8% in Arbagugu.
2. 73% were former tenants and 19% former own-cultivators.
3. 60% reported an increase in their cultivated area and 31% a decrease in cultivated area.
4. 60% consider wheat and barley to be their primary crops.

A farmer who lives in Asella RDC, Chilalo Awraja, represented a large number of the respondents with the above characteristics. He is a former evicted tenant and cultivates 2 ha. His major crops are wheat and barley. He reported an increase in his cultivatable land since 1975, and feels secure about the long-term tenure of his land. He has invested in his farm by buying oxen and a dairy cow. He is a regular credit participant. He has used 100 kg. of fertilizer every year since 1975, and he indicated an increase in both his income and agricultural output.

During further investigation of the respondents who reported a decrease in income, the following patterns were observed:

1. A number of them, particularly those in Chilalo, were former owner-cultivators whose cultivated land decreased substantially after 1975.
2. A considerable number of them lived in lowland and major livestock areas. The majority of the respondents who live in the lowland area and reported a decrease in income consider maize and sorghum to be their primary crop. ARDU's adaptive research and extension activity for maize and sorghum is very limited. Hence, it is unlikely that there would be an improvement in

production among farmers who cultivate these crops. The reason for a decrease in income in predominatly livestock areas may be that milk collection and marketing was transferred from ARDU's jurisdiction to the Dairy Development Enterprise, a government parastatal. But the Dairy Development Enterprise only collects milk in areas close to major towns. This has substantially reduced milk marketing to urban areas from major milk-producing areas that are further away from urban areas. Consequently, farmers who derive a substantial part of their income from dairy production are likely to experience a decrease in their family income.

3. A considerable number of these respondents live in peasant associations that are affected by unpredictable rainfall patterns. For example, a number of farmers who lived in very hilly peasant associations experienced frequent crop failures due to flooding. Similarly, several farmers in the lowland zone indicated an absence of rainfall during the short rainy season (belg period) as a major factor affecting their productivity.

4. Farmers who consider teff the most important crop comprised the majority of the respondents with a decrease in agricultural output but with an increase in income. This is because the price of teff since 1976 has increased at a greater rate than the price of other grains, even wheat.

The study, as mentioned previously, did not ask for a specific figure on household income. As a result, the findings from this survey cannot be compared with those of other surveys. The average income of farmers in Arsi is believed to have increased since 1975. The 1980 ARDU survey showed an increase in the average income per rural household from 875 birr before the Agrarian Reform to 1,647.16 birr after the Agrarian Reform in Chilalo; from 765.65 birr to 1,378.80 birr in Ticho and from 639 to 1,352.45 birr in Arbagugu. (8) While this suggests that there has been a substantial increase in income in all Awrajas, these figures must be treated with caution. As the 1980 survey points out income from sale of animals is derived by taking the weekly income and changing it to a yearly income by multiplying it by 52. (9) Given the nature of a rural economy, where income flows are seasonal and prone to fluctuation, the extrapolation from the weekly to yearly income is likely to compound any bias in the weekly figure. Hence, this method of estimating income is unreliable.

In consideration of farmers' reluctance to reveal their true income, the study posed more subtle questions about items or living conditions which are often used as indicators of wealth, such as the possession of a radio or a tin roof. Both are relatively expensive items in rural Ethiopia.

Table 27

Comparison of "Unobtrusive" Indicators of Income Between Surveys

Type of Survey	Respondents With Radio (%)	Respondents With Tin Roof (%)
1980 ARDU Survey	29.23	14.28
1984 Dejene Survey	30.00	22.00

With regard to these *unobtrusive* indicators, the results of the two surveys are similar, except that by 1984 slightly more farmers had tin roofs.

This suggests, on the one hand, that the substantial increase in income as reported by the 1980 survey is likely to be correct. On the other hand, it raises doubts about the 1980 figure (but does not disprove it) since this survey shows more respondents with tin roofs but not with a substantial an increase in income as in the 1980 survey. The only other information in this regard is the 1981 ARDU evaluation. The members of the evaluation team reported no improvement in the standard of living in Arsi since 1975. (10)

In an attempt to analyze the variables which may have influenced income, a component of one of the research question, income was cross-tabulated with: (a) major occupation, (b) literacy, (c) advice received on crop improvement, (d) advice received on livestock improvement, (e) agricultural production, (f) change in size of cultivated area, (g) marketing arrangement, and (h) housing conditions. The results displayed a statistically significant relationship between income and advice received on crop improvement, agricultural production, size of cultivated area and improvement in housing.

Forty-seven percent of the sampled farmers received advice on crop improvement. They made up the largest group (50%) with increased income. On the other hand, 60% of those who did not receive advice on crop improvement indicated a decrease in income. As pointed out earlier, advice on crop improvement concerned primarily the use of fertilizer and improved seed. The implementation of the measures suggested brought a significant increase in wheat and barley production to a majority of farmers in the sample group. Thus, the statistical relationship between income and advice received on crop improvement seems to be a logical one.

The majority of those who have not received advice on crops live in the Ti-cho and Arbagugu Awrajas. They do not use fertilizer, and 90% of them have not seen an ARDU extension agent. This suggests two important hypotheses:

1. Farmers who use fertilizer are likely to have higher incomes, since advice on crops essentially consists of access to fertilizer;
2. Farmers who have no contact with ARDU extension agents are not using fertilizer and other new inputs. As a results, they did not see improvement in their incomes. This suggests that access to extension services indirectly contributes to an increase in income

There is a statistical relationship between change in size of cultivated area and change in income. The majority of the farmers (58%), reported an increase in income as well as an increase in their size of cultivated area. Similarly, the majority of farmers (57%), who indicated a decrease in income also reported a decrease in the size of cultivated area. A closer examination of the 58% of farmers with increased income and cultivated area and the 57% with decreased income and decreased cultivated area revealed conflicting patterns. On the one hand, the majority of the respondents with increased income were from the more fertile and high wheat-producing regions in all the three Awrajas. On the other hand, although fewer in number, there were respondents from fertile areas who indicated a decrease in income. Peasant associations in these fertile areas are experiencing land pressure as more members are joining without a simultaneous expansion of cultivatable land. Land in these areas is intensively cultivated; soil fertility is gradually declining because of over-crowding, over-grazing and parceling of land.

One farmer who belongs to one of the peasant associations presently undergoing land shortage was interviewed during the course of this study. He lives in Etheya RDC, in a Peasant association of 560 ha. and 260 members. He is 30 years old and has 3 children. He owns 1 ha. of land and cultivates all of it. His holding is divided into two parcels. In 1975 his total land holding was 2 ha., with the decrease attributable to land adjustments in his PA. Land for grazing is a serious problem in this peasant association and there has been a decline in soil fertility because of intensive cultivation. Ten years ago this farmer fallowed his land but did not apply fertilizer; at present he uses fertilizer. Yet he thinks that his output was just as high then as it is now. He fears that his share of land may decrease in the future as more members join his peasant association. If this happens, he says, the decrease in productivity and income he has "experienced in the last few years will worsen."

E. Savings

It is generally agreed that the mobilization of savings from rural households is an important factor in the development of less developed countries who rely heavily on agriculture. Even if there is an increase in a farmer's income, the increment should be channeled in a productive way to promote capital accumulation.

The study appraised the savings ability of farmers. Farmers were asked if they had any money left after buying foodstuffs, manufactured goods, agricultural inputs, and other household expenses, after paying taxes. Only 7% of the sampled farmers have savings. The rest do not have cash savings. The specific amount of farmers' savings was not asked. Farmers are reluctant to reveal the amount of savings they have, fearing demands for taxes and contributions. Moreover, the idea behind the question is to give a sense of whether or not farmers have some cash after the end of the agricultural season. It should be noted that savings does not mean investment. There are farmers with no savings but who had made some investment in their farms.

The 1980 ARDU survey also indicated the remarkably low savings capacity of sampled farmers (7% with savings) in Arsi. Most farmers are likely to consume all of their income. This may be because farmers do not believe that they will receive higher returns from savings and investment. Further research on the factors affecting the average propensity to save is most relevant to the overall objective of increasing peasant production.

F. Social Services

One of the greatest achievements of the Agrarian Reform is the improvement in social services to the rural population. Specifically, it has tried to promote education, health, water supply, and rural roads.

1. Access to Education

In 1974 the total enrollment at the primary school level (1-6 grade) in Ethiopia was 859,831. By 1981 it had reached 1,119,729, with an annual growth of 21 percent. This dramatically improved the participation rate at the primary school level from 18 percent in 1974 to 43 percent in 1981. (11) Primary school attendance is likely to be higher in Arsi, as it is one of the more prosperous regions. The findings of this study support this argument; 96 percent of the respondents said that access to education for their children has improved. It is most likely that more resources have been devoted to expanding the number of primary schools and teachers to increase attendance.

Literacy rate for Arsi before the Agrarian Reform was about 9%; this survey indicated a 23% literacy rate. Among the sampled households 7% indicated that their wives could read and write. All the women who are supposed literate and 89% of the men claiming literacy had learned through the Adult Literacy Campaigns strongly promoted by the government since the Agrarian Reform. These findings offer evidence that the government's efforts are having some success.

2. Access to Clinics

A large number of the respondents who felt that access to clinics has remained about the same since 1975 lived in the Chilalo Awraja where the region's CADU program took an active interest in public health. CADU provided health services until 1971, when that function was transferred to the Ministry of Public Health. During that time CADU collaborated in undertaking studies with the Ethiopian Nutrition Institute. CADU studies have promoted a better understanding of rural health problems and sensitized the government to the importance of preventive health care services, especially maternal and child care and family planning. (12)

Of the 37% who indicated an improvement in health services, the majority lived in the Ticho and Arbagugu Awrajas. This does not imply that health services are better in these awrajas than in Chilalo. It suggests that the remote areas in these awrajas, such as Seru RDC in Ticho and Guna RDC in Arbagugu, did not have any access to clinics prior to 1974. Thus, they are more likely to feel the impact of change.

3. Housing Conditions

The majority of the respondents (62%) reported that their housing conditions are the same as prior to the Agrarian Reform, 27% said they have improved, and 11% said they have deteriorated. There is a statistically significant relationship between improvement in housing and family income. On further examination of the 41 respondents whose housing conditions have improved, it was found that 9 of the respondents (22%) earn the same income as prior to the Agrarian Reform, 24 of them (59%) have increased their income, and 8 of them (20%) are earning less income. Hence, it is valid to maintain that an increase in income has led to an improvement in housing conditions.

Further investigation of the respondents with improved housing conditions (27%) revealed that the majority of them live close to towns with good roads. A large number of them reported seeing an extension agent in the past year. They have also invested in their farms. Half of these respondents attribute the idea of their investment to ARDU agents. Thus it is plausible to argue that ARDU extension programs may have influenced their decisions to improve their housing conditions.

4. Water Supply

Eighty percent of the respondents reported that access to drinking water is the same as prior to the Agrarian Reform while 20% reported an improvement. During the CADU period high priority was given to conducting water development studies for both human and livestock consumption. CADU developed a master plan to build wells for storing rainwater and to drill boreholes, with the local community bearing part of the construction cost. ARDU is currently involved in self-help water supply construction ventures in which ARDU covers 25% of the construction costs and local farmers cover the remaining 75%. Under this scheme, ARDU constructs boreholes and micro-dams and diverts rivers for irrigation and drinking water. But most communities find the 75% local contribution too high. ARDU is trying to get the government to reduce it to 50%.

One of the major reasons why the majority of the respondents (83%) feel that there has been no improvement in drinking water is that most of ARDU's efforts are concentrated upon towns. This survey was conducted among rural households; thus it is likely to exclude the major beneficiaries of the ARDU water system.

The findings from this survey on the source of drinking water are compared to those of the 1980 ARDU survey in Table 28. (13)

Table 28

Comparison of Source of Drinking Water in Arsi

Type of Survey	Respondents' Source of Drinking Water (%)			
	Spring	River	ARDU Borehole	Water Pond
1980 ARDU Survey 1984	15.68	61.17	4.17	19.85
Dejene Survey	22.00	46.00	10.00	22.00

The findings from both surveys suggest that rivers provide the primary source of drinking water among sampled farmers in Arsi.

The safest drinking water is from boreholes drilled by ARDU. Yet only 10% of the respondents from this survey and 4.17% from the 1980 survey had access to them. All the farmers' who obtain water from boreholes also indicated an improvement in drinking water; and all lived in the Chilalo Awraja. There were areas covered by this study where boreholes were installed but not functioning. Lack of spare parts and technical and managerial skills prevented the operation from functioning smoothly.

ARDU's water improvement strategy is town-based. Hence, this program effectively excludes rural farm families, who must travel long distances to town to use ARDU's water. Consequently, rivers and watering ponds are the source of drinking water for the majority of the respondents in both the 1980 ARDU and this survey. Drinking water from rivers and watering ponds which are also used by animals endangers human health. Thus, unless the ARDU strategy becomes more rural and community based, its contribution toward improving drinking water for the majority of the rural population will continue to be minimal.

5. Rural Roads

The fact that sixty-five percent of the respondents felt that rural road conditions have improved is an indication of the success of ARDU's efforts to build roads. CADU played a major role in laying the ground work for the improvement of rural roads and ARDU has continued with these efforts.

Before the arrival of CADU in 1968, only two all-weather roads existed in Arsi, both in Chilalo Awraja. CADU planners realized that linking communities tall-weather roads is critical to successful extension services and the marketing of farmers' agricultural products. In 1972 CADU administered a plan to link five important villages to all-weather roads, and ARDU continued the road construction with the participation of the local people. In the construction of feeder roads, like water supply improvements, the beneficiaries bear 75% of the cost. Since 1975 ARDU has constructed 177 km. of roads at the request of local communities. Some of them included linking the remote areas of Ticho and Arbagugu to Chilalo.

While a larger number of farmers in Ticho and Arbagugu than in Chilalo indicated an improvement in road conditions, the roads in Ticho and Arbagugu are not in better condition than those in Chilalo. On the contrary, until the recent reconstruction by ARDU, the main roads Ticho and Arbagugu Awrajas (especially Arbagugu) were inaccessible during the rainy season. Some Weredas in Ticho and Arbagugu are still extremely difficult to reach by car. Consequently, farmers in Ticho and Arbagugu experienced a more dramatic improvement in rural roads since 1975.

G. Credit Participation

The availability of agricultural credit to small farmers who have little or no capital (or savings) to invest in farming is an important component in small farm development projects. Credit can raise land and labor productivity by providing modern agricultural inputs like fertilizer, seed, insecticides, and improved tools.

CADU, through its marketing division, offered credit in kind for eligible farmers to obtain fertilizer, improved seed, pesticides and herbicides, agricultural implements, and pregnant cross-bred heifers. Fertilizer, which accounted for 94% of the credit sales, was the single most important commodity in the credit program. (15)

ARDU offers credit to farmers to buy inputs through service cooperatives and the peasant association. The number of regular and irregular credit participants is shown in Table 29.

Table 29

Comparison of Surveys of Credit Participation in Arsi

Source of Credit	Percentage of Credit Participants			
	Chilalo	Ticho	Arbagugu	Arsi
1980 ARDU Survey (regular)				
	79.47	56.02	59.88	69.68
1984 Dejene Survey (regular and irregular participants)				
	82.00	54.00	53.00	70.00
1984 ARDU Report				
	-	-	-	38.00

In 1975/76, 23% of households were participating in credit schemes. Using the same report and household figure, the number of credit participants rose to 38% in 1984. (16) The 1980 ARDU survey found that 69.98% received regular credit in Arsi. (17) From the above comparison, it is reasonable to conclude that the number of credit participants has substantially increased since 1975.

However, the 1984 ARDU report figure on credit participants is more credible than either the author's figure or that of the 1980 survey. ARDU borrows from the Agricultural and Industrial Development Bank and has to repay it. Hence, ARDU has a reliable record of credit participants. The present survey did not include a specific question on whether or not the farmer uses credit on a regular basis. As a result, the findings in this survey are likely to suggest the existence of more credit participants than others, which include only regular participants. It is likely, moreover, that both this survey and the 1980 ARDU survey may have sampling biases. Both include sampling areas which are high cereal-producing areas and where ARDU activities are strong. These areas have a much higher number of credit participants than others. Hence, the number of regular credit participants in both this survey and the 1980 survey is likely to be biased.

In both the 1980 and 1984 surveys, the level of credit participation in Chilalo was significantly higher than in Ticho and Arbagugu. This may be attributed to farmers' relatively higher stage of development in Chilalo, induced by CADU activity. It could also be due to a more effective extension program in Chilalo.

With the emergence of service cooperatives following the Agrarian Reform, ARDU has been gradually transferring the provision of credit to service cooperatives. Instead of ARDU's agents, these service cooperatives list the name of farmers who want to purchase fertilizer from each peasant association. The list is given to the AMC about six months in advance of the main planting season. The Ministry of Agriculture aggregates the total fertilizer demand for the nation and requests the Agricultural and Industrial Bank to give the loan to the AMC to buy the fertilizer. The AMC distributes the fertilizer to the service cooperatives. Individual farmers collect the fertilizer they have ordered from the service cooperatives by signing their credit loan. The credit is deducted when the farmers sell their produce to service cooperatives at the time of harvest.

Among the respondents who used credit, 76% indicated their source was the service cooperative. ARDU administrators transfer the provision of credit to a service cooperative only when they are sure that the respective service cooperative is prepared to carry out the task appropriately. These findings suggest that a large number of service cooperatives are administering credit in Arsi. This offers an indication of the relatively high stage of development of the service cooperative in Arsi as opposed to other regions of Ethiopia, where a lack of managerial accounting skills prevents successful administration of credit.

Further examination of the respondents who had not used credit reveals a statistical correlation according to Awraja. A significantly smaller number of respondents lived in Chilalo (18%) than in Ticho (46%) and Arbagugu (47%). The considerably higher number of respondents who do not use credit in Ticho and Arbagugu suggests much less use of fertilizer and improved seed in these awrajas than in Chilalo. Farmers in Chilalo are more exposed to agricultural inputs and are aware of the availability of credit to purchase them. This may be due to better extension services and active peasant associations in Chilalo.

The largest number of respondents purchased only fertilizer (71%). Among these respondents, 9% buy fertilizer either with cash from a service cooperative or from friends, relatives, or other farmers in their PAs (i.e., they do not use credit to buy their input).

Among the sampled farmers, 2% obtain improved seed only and 7% use both fertilizer and improved seed. The extremely low level of improved seed purchased among small farmers is also indicated in the 1980 ARDU survey, which reported that the number of respondents who took less than 2 quintals of improved seed increased from 2.79% in 1976 to 9.4% in 1978. In Ticho and Arbagugu, hardly any respondents bought improved seed. (18)

Although credit participation after 1975 has greatly increased, farmers use credit mainly to buy fertilizer. This should be of serious concern to ARDU, since the *combined* use of fertilizer and improved seed brings a substantial increase in output. In spite of the fact that ARDU produces about 25,000 qts. of improved seed for distribution annually, has one of the country's finest crop research stations and maintains seed multiplication farms at four different sites in Chilalo (19), most peasant farmers are not buying improved seed. The following factors offer possible explanations:

1. Discussions with ARDU extension agents revealed that the highest priority in the distribution of improved seed is given to producer cooperatives and then to registered service cooperatives.

2. The price of improved seed is exorbitantly high for most farmers. For a quintal of improved seed a farmer has to pay twice as much as what he would pay for a quint of wheat.

3. A considerable number of farmers are unimpressed by most varieties that they have tried because of loss of the original yield potential and a susceptibility to disease.

4. During interviews farmers indicated that they are multiplying and using the improved seed they bought over a decade ago under CADU.

In this section farmers were asked whether the amount of fertilizer consumption has increased or decreased since 1975. Slightly more respondents (40%) indicated an increase in the amount of fertilizer used than those who indicated a decrease (36%), and 24% said they use the same amount as prior to 1975. This increase may be due to the favorable conditions created for tenants after the reform, an increase in income and easier access to credit through the service cooperatives. However, it should be noted that those who indicated an increase used, on the average, 1 qt. of fertilizer. A number of them had never used fertilizer before the Agrarian Reform. While this survey did not ask how much fertilizer they apply per unit area, this is an important question for further research.

The 1980 ARDU survey also showed that the number of credit participants who are using up to 1 qt. of fertilizer has increased since 1975 in all awrajas. Yet the number of credit participants using from 1.5 - 2 qts. in all awrajas has not substantially changed. (20)

The respondents who indicated a decrease in the amount of fertilizer they use were asked to specify the reason for it (Table 30).

Table 30

Primary Reason for the Decreasing Application of Fertilizer

Reason for Decreasing Use of Fertilizer	# Interviewed	% Interviewed
Increasing Fertilizer Price	20	47
Fertilizer was Unavailable on Time	10	23
Cultivatable Area Has Decreased	8	19
Lack of Money to Buy Fertilizer	2	5
Afraid of Risk	3	6
Total	43	100

The majority of the respondents (47%) cited increasing fertilizer price as a primary reason for their decreasing use of fertilizer. The high price of fertilizer, particularly after 1979, was a disincentive to fertilizer use. What factors led to the dramatic increase in fertilizer prices which affected peasant farmers in Arsi?

1. International price: the international price for DAP fertilizer, which is used in Arsi, rose from $140/ton in 1978 to $193/ton in 1979. In 1980 it was $200/ton and has averaged $190/ton from 1981 to 1982. On the average, the international price in 1982/83 was 43 percent higher than the 1978/79 price. The price charged to farmers throughout Ethiopia, as in Chilalo Awraja, was about 100% percent above 1978/79 price. (21)
2. Domestic Policy: in 1979 the Ethiopian Government decided to import a large amount of fertilizer, exceeding the country's demand. The situation was exacerbated in 1980 by another purchase of over 100,100 tons of fertilizer. These large purchases led to a substantial increase in the internal cost structure - chiefly transportation and storage costs - which inflated the farmgate price for fertilizer. (22)

A 60-year-old farmer from a highland area in Chilalo (Sagure RDC) is a good representative of farmers who cited fertilizer price as their reason for decreasing fertilizer use. He was born a tenant and gradually bought land from his landlord to become an owner-cultivator. He has participated in CADU credit programs since 1970. Along with fertilizer, he received improved wheat seed from CADU which he still multiplies and uses on his own farm. During 1970-75 he bought 1 1/2 qt. of fertilizer for about 40 birr/qt. and from 1976-79 he bought 1 qt. of fertilizer for about 55 birr/qt. Since 1980 he reported cutting down his fertilizer usage to 1.2 qt. He said he could not afford the price of 85 birr/qt. in 1980/81 and 116 birr/qt. in 1981/82. He added that during this period there were a number of farmers in his PA who had abandoned the use of fertilizer.

The decrease in the amount of fertilizer purchased may also be attributed to lower grain prices, particularly relative to fertilizer prices. The government has kept an artificially low price for wheat and barley. This affects the purchasing power of farmers.

ARDU also reported a decrease in the number of credit participants that were taking up to 1 qt. from 54.4% in 1978 to 43.4% in 1979 in Chilalo. (23) This is probably the result of increasing fertilizer prices.

Among the respondents who had never used fertilizer 11% lived in Chilalo, 37% in Ticho and 37% in Arbagugu Awraja. Through an examination of these respondents in Ticho and Arbagugu the following patterns seem to emerge:

1. Some of these respondents have not seen an ARDU extension agent nor are they aware of ARDU's credit program.
2. Some are aware that ARDU's credit program provides fertilizer (through their peasant association) but are afraid of the risk involved.

A 47-year-old Muslim with an eight member family in the lowland area of Arbagugu Awraja, may serve as an example of a farmer who fears the risk of using credit to buy fertilizer. His total landholdings, all of which he cultivates, equal 1.5 hectares. He belongs to a PA with an area of 680 ha., and 162 members. Sorghum and maize (which he uses for consumption) are his most important crops. Although he is aware of the availability of credit for fertilizer purchases, he is reluctant to use it. He is afraid that he will not be able to pay back his credit since bad harvests occur in this lowland area frequently due to lack of rain. This peasant is an example of the type of farmer with low productivity and savings that is familiar to readers of the literature on credit in developing countries.

Small farmers in Arsi, as well as throughout Ethiopia, must indicate a year in advance whether they want to buy fertilizer. Since peasant agriculture depends on rainfall, small farmers with limited resources and low productivity are reluctant to use credit to buy inputs. This phenomenon is even more widespread in other regions of Ethiopia where the majority of farmers have subsistence-level output.

Farmers were further asked whether they had easier access to credit after the Agrarian Reform. Among the sampled farmers, 86% had no trouble obtaining credit, and 80% considered the interest rate to be fair. This suggests greater availability of credit to smallholders since the Agrarian Reform. However, 39% of the respondents indicated that they have trouble obtaining fertilizer at the right time due to a delay in the delivery of fertilizer to their peasant association. Table 30 also shows that the second largest number of respondents (23%) cited this as a reason for decreased use of fertilizer. Lack of repayment of credit by some members of their peasant association was the single most important reason cited for the delay in fertilizer delivery by farmers.

In 1979 the Ethiopian Government gave peasant associations the responsibility of collecting credit repayments. However, a peasant association cannot be granted credit for inputs until 95% of the previous year's debts are paid. As a result of this requirement, there are a number of instances when farmers who had paid their credit did not receive their fertilizer on time because others had failed to pay on time.

H. Farm Implements

This survey attempted to find whether there has been a change in the kinds of farm implements used by peasant farmers since 1975, and if the change is a result of ARDU's program. Before presenting these findings, a brief summary of CADU/ARDU activity on this issue is appropriate.

Under CADU, the Agricultural Engineering Section undertook research to improve traditional methods of seedbed preparation, crop handling, and on-farm transportation. The basic objective was to produce farm implements which would be labor intensive and within the purchasing capacity of the small farmers.

Among important innovations made available to farmers were:

1. The design of the mould board plough, which is ox-drawn. It is intended to replace the traditional metal-tipped wooden plow. It is more efficient in reducing weed growth and covering more crop residue. The advantage of this tool is that it reduces both the farmer and oxen labor in ploughing and seedbed preparation.
2. The design of the spike-tooth harrow, also ox-drawn. Trials at CADU with the improved harrow resulted in a more uniform covering of seeds and therefore in better germination and higher plant population per unit area. This

tool has been shown to reduce substantially the working hours on the farm required by the traditional method.

3. A thresher to replace the traditional method of oxen trampling the grain on the floor. The traditional threshing method is very slow and very demanding of oxen that may not have enough feed since this takes place during the long dry season. The thresher, which costs about 3,000 Eth. birr, is quite expensive for the average farmer.

4. Wheel barrows and ox-drawn carts, developed for various transportation purposes. (24)

Since the expansion of CADU into ARDU, the same function has continued but under the name of the Agricultural Implement and Industry Promotion Department. In addition to the improved farm implements already mentioned, ARDU develops donkey-carts, bee hives and various home furnishings.

This usage of farm implements among the overwhelming number of sampled farmers (96%) has not changed since the Agrarian Reform. Only (4%) are using improved implements developed by ARDU. All of them live in Chilalo Awraja. A number of them were a "model farmer" under CADU's extension scheme and had purchased the implement before the Agrarian Reform.

The improved implement used by most farmers in Chilalo is an improved harrow. During the interview these farmers also indicated that they had learned about improved harrows at demonstrations held on the *model farmer* farm under CADU. The cost of the improved harrow is relatively low, and the tool is reported to be suitable for local farming conditions. Such findings suggest that there has been little improvement in the level of farm technology among farmers in Arsi since 1975. The 1980 ARDU survey, like the present one, revealed that the dissemination of ARDU's improved implements among peasant farmers was very limited. (25)

The reasons why 96% of the respondents were not using the farm implements developed by ARDU are presented in Table 31.

Table 31

Reasons for Not Using Farm Implements Developed by ARDU

Reason for not Using ARDU's Farm Implements	# Interviewed	% Interviewed
Doesn't Know About The Equipment	92	64
Equipment is Expensive	26	18
Difficult to Handle	10	7
Heavy for the Ox to Carry the Equipment	6	4
Equipment is not Suitable for the Land	8	6
Hasn't Received the Equipment He Wanted to Buy	2	1
Total	144	100

The results of Table 31 clearly underline the extremely low performance of ARDU in regard to the dissemination of information about farm implements, since 64% of the respondents did not even know about improved implements developed by ARDU. This is another example that illustrates ARDU's haphazard method in the delivery of its extension services.

Before the Agrarian Reform (under CADU) 84 oxen carts, 1400 harrows, 730 ploughs, 400 hoes, and 16 threshers were developed as opposed to 36 oxen carts, 12 donkey carts, 28 harrow, and no hoes and threshers after the Reform. (26) This confirms ARDU's low performance in developing improved implements since the Agrarian Reform. Thus, a commitment by ARDU to concentrate its research and extension efforts on the development of appropriate and easy-to-handle equipment, which is at the same time affordable to the majority of the small farmers in the Arsi region, is vital. This would also have a broader national significance since there is hardly any improvement in the level of farming technology in other regions of Ethiopia.

Notes

1. *Arsi Rural Development Unit: Objectives, Activities, Impact, Prospects and Problems*, Asella: Ethiopia, 1984, p. 5.

2. *Investigation of the Impact of the Agrarian Reform on Peasants' Income and Expenditure Patterns, 1980*, Asella: Ethiopia, ARDU Publication No. 18, 1981, p. 26.

3. *Arsi Rural Development Unit: Objectives, Activities, Impact, Prospects and Problems*, Asella: Ethiopia, 1984, p. 14.

4. *Arsi Rural Development Unit: Objectives, Activities, Impact, Prospects and Problems*, Asella: Ethiopia, 1984, p. 17.

5. *IBID*, p. 17

6. Obtained from the Regional Office of The All Ethiopian Peasant Association in Asella, May, 1984.

7. Carl Linbald and Laurel Druban, *Small Farm Grain Storage*, Action/Peace Crops 1976, p. 3.

8. *Investigation on the Impact of the Agrarian Reform in peasants' Income and Expenditure Patterns, 1980*, Asella: Ethiopia, ARDU Publication No. 18, 1981. p. 29.

9. *IBID*, p. 53.

10. Solomon Bekure et al, *Evaluation of the Arsi Rural Development Unit, 1981*, Uppsala: Swedish University of Agricultural Science, September 1981, p.(I:4).

11. *Some Explanatory Notes on Educational Development in Ethiopia*, Addis Ababa: Ethiopia, September 1981, p. 16.

12. *Family Guidance in the CADU Program*, 1970, CADU Publications No. 62, 1971.

13. *Investigation of the Impact of the Agrarian Reform on Peasants' Income and Expenditure Patters, 1980*, Asella: Ethiopia, ARDU Publication No. 18, 1981, p. 29.

14. *Arsi Rural Development Unit"Objectives, Activities, Impact, Prospects and Problems*, Asella: Ethiopia, 1984, p. 7.

15. John Holmberg, "The Credit Program of CADU in Ethiopia," *Small Farm Credit in Ethiopia*, Washington, D.C., USAID, Vol. 8, 1973, p. 15.

16. *Arsi Rural Development Unit: Objectives, Activities, ARDU* Publication No. 18, 1981, p. 12-13.

17. *Investigation of the Impact of the Agrarian Reform on peasants' Income and Expenditure Patterns, 1980*, Asella: Ethiopia, ARDU Publication No. 18, 1981, p. 11.

18. *IBID*, p. 13.

136

19. *Arsi Rural Development Unit: Objectives, Activities, Impact, Prospects and Problems*, Asella: Ethiopia, 1984.

20. *Investigation on the Impact of the Agrarian Reform in Peasants' Income and Expenditure Patterns, 1980*, Asella: Ethiopia, ARDU Publication no. 18, 1981, p. 12-13.

21. *The World Bank, Economic Analysis and Projections Department*, Washington, D.C.: 1983, pp. 26-27.

22. *Ethiopia: Review of Farmers' Incentives and Agricultural Marketing and Distribution Efficiency*, Washington, D.C.: The World Bank, 1983, pp. 30-35.

23. *Investigation of the Impact of the Agrarian Reform on Peasants' Income and Expenditure Patterns, 1980*, Asella: Ethiopia, ARDU Publication No. 18, 1981, p. 12.

24. *CADU, Implement Research Station*, Asella: Ethiopia, Progress Report No. 2, CADU Publication No. 53, 1970.

25. *Investigation of the Impact of the Agrarian Reform on Peasants' Income and Expenditure Patterns, 1980*, Asella: Ethiopia, ARDU Publication No. 18, 1981, p. 77.

26. *CADU Annual Report, 1971/72 and 1972/73*, CADU Publication No. 77, Asella: Ethiopia, 1983, p. 13. See also: *ARDU Annual Report, 1981/82*, ARDU Publication No. 22, Asella: Ethiopia.

Chapter 7

Conclusion: Strategies for Growth and for Social Transformation

This study analyzed peasant farmers' perceptions of the emerging peasant institutions, government agencies, and rural development efforts in the Arsi region. An analysis of this kind provides valuable insights into the strategies, policies, and research studies that could stimulate peasant agricultural production in Ethiopia.

Several studies have identified one of the major obstacles to promoting agricultural growth in Ethiopia as a lack of surplus generated by, and invested in, the peasant sector. (1) This surplus is unlikely to be attained through individual farming under a peasant association given the adverse conditions they face currently in Ethiopia. For instance, the findings from this study have shown that all of the following factors inhibit the effectiveness of the extension and government services: decreasing size of cultivated area, fragmented holdings, limited availability of fertilizer and improved seed, lack of improvement in farming technology and access to draft animals, land degradation, poor storage facilities, and lack of all-weather roads. Under these conditions, individual farmers cannot generate investable surplus for development.

Yet, at present, the majority of the sample group of farmers in Arsi (75%) would like to remain smallholders within the peasant association while only 25% are interested in joining producer cooperatives. The preference shown by most peasant farmers to remain smallholders is also reported to be common to peasants in other regions of Ethiopia. Their choice contradicts the government's objective to gradually transform the system of individual farming into collective farming under the producer cooperative.

The current government policy suffers from one basic flaw; extension agents and government officers induce farmers to join producer cooperatives on the assumption that large-scale agriculture is superior to small-scale individual farming in terms of over-all productivity. As witnessed during the field study, this view is also reiterated by high-level government officials and field-level extension agents who disseminate this idea to peasant farmers. Yet, farmers in most producer cooperatives do not have significantly higher yields or incomes than those who are smallholders in a peasant association. As a result, most farmers are not tempted to join producer cooperatives.

This government policy has also led to a premature establishment of producer cooperatives in areas that are not even suited for large-scale mechanized agriculture. Furthermore, the principle motivation of most farmers who join is that the cooperative provides greater access to oxen and government services. Some producer cooperatives have introduced tractors without possessing adequate technical and financial capabilities; this has resulted in heavy dependence upon the assistance of the Ministry of Agriculture.

The cornerstone of the government's policy to promote the cooperative movement should be its ability to mobilize the under-utilized and abundant labor in the peasant sector. This fundamental advantage is made evident through the examination of service cooperatives in Arsi. At present, however, the emphasis of the cooperative movement is on introducing collective farming through the establishment of producer cooperatives. This policy has greatly contributed to the peasants' negative attitude towards cooperativisation in general, and producer cooperatives in particular. Thus, the government's priority, the establishment of producer cooperatives, even when the country is still at a stage of development in which the full benefits of cooperative efforts cannot be reaped, seems misplaced and is likely to be counter-productive to the government's own objective. In fact, one of the major factors contributing to the strength of the model producer cooperatives discussed in Chapter 4 was the primacy given to cooperative efforts.

The field investigation in Arsi indicated that service cooperatives have become the most effective institutions for mobilizing resources and labor and promoting production enterprises that have greatly improved the welfare of the rural population. Using local resources and pooling the labor of its members, service cooperatives are involved in building schools, clinics, and rural roads, installing potable water, and undertaking reforestation and soil water conservation projects. A considerable number of the service cooperatives in Arsi have made rapid progress far beyond the government's expectations and are providing services such as flour and oil mills, storage facilities, dairy farms, cottage industries, and rental of farm machinery.

The performance and the popularity of service cooperatives among most farmers warrants the government to reconsider its policy of establishing producer cooperatives immediately. At present, the government's financial and manpower investment is concentrated on strengthening producer cooperatives. For example, farmers in producer cooperatives pay low prices for fertilizer and minimal land tax, and receive interest-free loans and higher prices for grain. Moreover, extension agents spend most of their time assisting farmers in producer cooperatives rather than small farmers. Such a heavy investment has not achieved a significant improvement ie. increasing yields or generating savings among farmers in producer cooperatives. Hence, it seems appropriate to redirect efforts to strengthen service cooperatives which promise to be the most effective institutional framework for attaining growth and promoting the cooperative movement.

The emphasis of the cooperative movement should be on the sharing and management of the productive resources which farmers presently lack. For instance, the Agrarian Reform has not addressed the problem of unequal access to draft animals; and approximately half of the peasant farmers in Ethiopia have either one or no oxen. Since ploughing in Ethiopia is done by two oxen, most of these farmers rent or exchange labor services for the use of oxen. Through the collective ownership of oxen and farm implements under the service cooperative or peasant association, poor farmers could have access to oxen. This would help to overcome the single most serious obstacle to increasing cultivatable land, and, therefore agricultural production.

It was observed in Arsi that service cooperatives have an enormous potential to generate surplus capital through labor accumulation. Indeed, a number of service cooperatives in Arsi have now accumulated a large capital and are investing it in various income-generating activities. But the problem is that they cannot distribute the benefits directly to individual farmers. If service cooperatives had a mechanism to pay their members dividends, in some form, they would be likely to have even more popular support among the peasantry. Such an incentive mechanism would contribute to the generation of more surplus and to strengthening the cooperative movement in Ethiopia in general.

The other major obstacle most service cooperatives face is managerial and administrative inexperience; a lack of trained staff. Consequently, most service cooperatives in Ethiopia, except Arsi, are not able to cope adequately with the responsibility of grain marketing and the distribution of inputs, credits and consumer goods. Training programs in auditing, accounting, budgeting, bookkeeping, financial planning and consumer shop operation for selected staff of service cooperatives would greatly reduce their heavy reliance on the Ministry of Agriculture as well as enhance their role in the cooperative movement.

The dissatisfaction with service cooperatives expressed by a large number of farmers in Arsi centers around the areas of crop marketing and the distribution of consumer goods. As discussed in Chapter 5, service cooperatives have the ambivalent role of being an intermediary agency for the government to extract surplus from the peasantry. Peasant farmers are required to sell a certain quota of their produce to the Agricultural Marketing Corporation (AMC) through the service cooperatives. The price farmers receive is set by the AMC, the government parastatal, and is much lower than the AMC selling price. In addition, the share of consumer goods distributed by the Ethiopian Domestic Distribution Corporation (EDDC) to the peasant sector, through the service cooperatives, is very limited. This has contributed to the shortage of consumer goods in most rural areas. Consequently, low prices for agricultural products coupled by a shortage of consumer goods, are among the major disincentives to increasing the agricultural production of peasant farmers.

The inefficiency in the present marketing and distribution system, however, is not due to the service cooperatives. This problem stems largely from the dominant role the government parastatals, the AMC and EDDC, have in the economy. The capacity of these agencies, particularly that of the AMC, is extended to its limits while the private sector and service cooperatives are underutilized. Hence, these agencies have a high operating cost which leads to higher consumer prices for urban dwellers or even lower producer prices to farmers, as well as wide variations in farm-gate and selling prices which reduces farmers incentive for increased production. Furthermore, the situations tends to increase the black (parallel) market operation by merchants and has restricted the legitimate grain flows from surplus regions to food-deficit regions by private traders.

The strain on the AMC's role in grain marketing could be minimized by granting the right to service cooperatives to sell in the open market after they have sold certain quotas to the AMC. This is also likely to improve the price farmers receive for their produce and their motivation to increase marketed surplus. Most service cooperatives face problems pertaining to storage, transportation, cash flow, and management capability to undertake grain marketing operations. Efforts should be made to solve these problems before the role of service cooperatives is expanded to include some of the responsibilities normally handed by the AMC.

Increased availability of fertilizer and improved seed to peasant farmers is essential to substantially improve agricultural output over a relatively short period of time. The experience of Arsi farmers proves this fact. The major government institutions involved in credit and input supply are the Ministry of Agriculture, the Ministry of Domestic Trade, the Agricultural and Industrial Development Bank of Ethiopia, and the AMC. There is a serious lack of systematic coordination among these agencies, which has contributed to inefficiency and delayed availability of inputs to the peasant sector. None of these institutions have a direct linkage with credit borrowers, nor do they have the ultimate responsibility for the delivery of inputs to farmers or for procuring credits from farmers.

A large number of service cooperatives in Arsi have successfully assumed the responsibility of input distribution and credit management from ARDU. However, most service cooperatives in other regions of Ethiopia are too weak and inexperienced to undertake the task of input distribution and credit management. Their capacity to perform these tasks could be greatly strengthened by training a large number of staff members, by constructing storage facilities and by designing a mechanism that would create an effective linkage between the supply of agricultural inputs through credits in advance, and collecting the payment of these credits from the farmers' produce later on.

Gradually transferring some of the functions of input distribution and credit management to service cooperatives will also enable the Ministry of Agriculture staff to devote more of its time to the urgently needed task of disseminating agricultural technology. In addition, the government institutions seem to incur more capital and operating costs in the provision of inputs and credits as compared to when the same services are rendered in collaboration with service cooperatives. Service cooperatives are also able to recover the operating costs more easily than government institutions since they can generate it from the labor and financial contributions of their members.

The availability of credit to buy fertilizer has dramatically improved since the Agrarian Reform. Farmers attribute this to the establishment of peasant associations and service cooperatives. But what is also important to find out is whether the amount applied by individual farmers has been increasing or decreasing. It is reported that farmers on the average use considerably lower amounts of fertilizer than the amount recommended by the Ministry of Agriculture. Hence, the key questions for further research in this regard are (a) the average amount of fertilizer used by each household; and (b) whether fertilizer is used on a regular basis each year. The availability of credit to purchase inputs is only one side of the equation. Its regular use and the amount applied per unit area are also important factors.

At the moment, service cooperatives are small and isolated institutions that are trying to fill the void created by the substantial reduction of the private sector's involvement in agriculture following the Ethiopian Revolution. In order to be effective in the areas of crop marketing, and input and credit supply, they need to be organized into a higher form of union at the Wereda, Awraja, and national level, as is the peasant association. This has been a major issue of debate between donor agencies and the Ethiopian government. The Ethiopian government is reluctant to establish such a cooperative union. But such a union could be directed by a government institution. The advantage of such a union is that it could address some of the problems in grain marketing and the distribution of consumer goods that are caused by the monopoly of the government parastatal. For instance, the cooperative union at the national level, could transport grain to the AMC or urban markets directly. It could also collect inputs from the AMC and consumer goods from the EDDC to distribute to the service cooperatives at the village level.

The potential of service cooperatives to mobilize rural women in its development efforts is impeded by the exclusion of women and women's associations from service cooperative membership. Under the current system, the women's associations make financial contributions to service cooperatives. Yet they neither participate in the credit program nor receive much benefit from the service cooperatives, except for access to the cooperative shop. For example, as observed in Arsi, the dairy farm enterprise has not involved any women despite the woman's traditional role in animal husbandry. Hence, a mechanism to integrate women's associations into the structure of the service cooperative and promote production and income-generating enterprises that meet the need of rural women, will enhance their contribution to increased productivity as well as improve the welfare of their families.

The findings from Arsi indicate that decreasing cultivatable land among rural households, land tenure insecurity, lack of improvement in farm implements, and lack of adoption of improved technologies, are fundamental problems limiting the productivity of peasant farmers. These problems are even more pronounced in other regions of Ethiopia where the uncertainty of rainfall and soil degradation and deforestation are severe. In such an unfavorable environment farmers are unlikely to take risk of adopting new technologies or making some form of farm investment.

The Agrarian Reform has not made any change in the average landholding of peasant farmers in Ethiopia. Without an increase in cultivatable land, intensive cultivation, over-grazing and over-crowding will become increasingly serious problems in many of the relatively fertile regions of Ethiopia. Eventually these conditions will lead to environmental degradation, deforestation and soil erosion, making the land vulnerable to drought. One of the major reasons for the decreasing amount of cultivatable land is the frequent land adjustment undertaken by the peasant association because of changing family size. These adjustments have also contributed to fragmented holdings. The shortage of cultivatable land has serious implications for the strategies to improve peasant production; and further research in this area is is urgently needed. The findings of this study suggest two central questions to be explored: (1) how could a peasant association expand its total landholding, and (2) would it be possible to design a process that would minimize the frequent land redistribution that leads to smaller plot size and fragmentation to an extent where it becomes inefficient to use modern inputs.

A major way of expanding cultivatable area is to provide access to oxen and use a labor intensive scheme for recovering land with poor fertility and drainage problems. The ox used for ploughing and harvesting is the most important animal in Ethiopian agriculture and yet half of the nations farmers do not own the pair needed to cultivate their land. A system of sharing oxen with those who do not have any would intensify cultivation through labor mobilization; this could be easily undertaken by the service cooperatives and peasant associations. Cultivatable land could also be increased by reducing the amount of land left fallow to maintain soil fertility. Soil maintenance could be attained through improved agricultural practices such as crop rotation and intensive use of fertilizer.

Research on livestock has consistently failed to notice one of the critical needs of farmers in Arsi: the improvement of oxen. The emphasis of research has been on the improvement of dairy cattle. This is an important activity, to be sure, and it has increased milk production in Arsi. But the animal breeding program should give oxen improvement higher priority.

Shortage of land for grazing is becoming a serious problem in Arsi as well as in other regions of Ethiopia. As the average cultivatable land per household decreases, the problem of over-grazing is likely to worsen thereby contributing to land degradation. Introducing improved pasture and fodder crops through the coordinated efforts of the extension program and research institutions and the establishment of communal grazing land are ways of dealing with this problem.

The 1975 Agrarian Reform founded a system in which all rural families have use of cultivatable land without private ownership. It is not the absence of private ownership that is the major reason for land tenure insecurity among most peasant farmers in Arsi. Rather, land insecurity is caused by frequent land adjustments conducted by the peasant association; adjustments which have for the most part reduced the size of the area cultivated by most farmers, and produced the fear that the government, who, they feel ultimately owns the land, will ask them to join producer cooperatives. Farmers' land insecurity reduces their desire to invest in their farm as well as their incentive to increase their production.

The extension service in Arsi, as in other regions of Ethiopia, does not reach the village level directly, does not transmit information in a systematic way, and does not conduct regular visits to farmers. The extension agents are more heavily involved in district planning, cooperative promotion, and political education than they are in disseminating agricultural innovation. It's programs are focused more on those farmers who belong in producer cooperatives than on the smallholder. As a result, the extension service is not effective in meeting the needs of smallholders.

The generation of new technologies through agricultural research has been extremely limited. This is due to the following reasons: (a) variation in agroecological zones of areas in close proximity to one another that makes the generation of site specific technologies difficult; (b) limited manpower and commitment to research; (c) lack of systematic contact between research and extension; and (d) lack of the flow of information from farmers to researchers, and from researchers to farmers. Unless these problems are addressed, research cannot be as relevant to farmers' needs nor bring a substantial increase in yields among farmers at a faster rate. For instance, the absence of a feedback mechanism among farmers, extension agents and researchers has resulted in the ineffectiveness of the herbicide and pesticide given to farmers in Arsi; farmers indicated that the pesticides they use against rats and the herbicides they use against weeds are not effective in preventing crop losses, yet they receive the same advice and chemicals every year.

At present, most of the research has focused on crop improvement, particularly on wheat. This is as true in Arsi as it is in other regions of Ethiopia. The success in increasing the production and income of farmers in Arsi is largely due to the dissemination of high-yielding wheat and barley along with fertilizer. The success of these crops was important in gaining the confidence of the farmers. But wheat and barley crops are ecologically well-adapted to most of the highland and medium altitude zones in Arsi. Adaptive research on teff, sorghum and maize is seriously lacking even in Arsi, which has one of the finest plant husbandry departments in the country. Sorghum and maize are particularly important crops in the lowland areas of Ethiopia and should be given high priority in the development of research projects.

The emphasis in research on high-yielding crops like wheat should be pursued cautiously. Unlike the Asian countries, where there is a proven agricultural technology to extend and where farmers rely heavily on irrigation systems, Ethiopian agriculture is predominantly rainfed and farmers operate with a relatively high risk production factor. The concern of most peasant farmers is not only to increase their yields but also to secure enough yields for family consumption. Thus the single crop research strategy should be shifted towards farming system research in which inter-croping and livestock improvement are significant strategies for increasing the productivity of farmers.

Farming system research examines the complex interaction between man, plant, animal and the soil conditions and makes an effort to promote technologies which are suitable to agro-ecological variations. (2) It would involve increasing the role of farmers in research by conducting more experimental trials on fields cultivated by actual farmers than the usual research station does. It would also include farmers while testing the experimental trials. An example of the absence of valuable farming system research was noted in Arsi when the problem of water availability was neglected during the introduction of new innovations in Ethiopia.

Peasant agriculture in Ethiopia is essentially rainfed. Drought due to lack of adequate rainfall is a major cause of periodic famine in Ethiopia. Hence, water should be considered to be an important factor in the improvement of agricultural productivity. As witnessed during the field work, inputs like fertilizer and improved seed are useless in the absence of rain. In fact, the sustained availability of a water supply (through irrigation or ground water sources) will be a major factor if a substantial increase in agricultural productivity is to occur in Ethiopia. Needless to say, research on the supply and distribution of water is crucial. Such research, combined with an effort to increase the water retention capacity of the soil through improved farming practices, would yield a return equal to that obtained through other inputs. If the problem of rainfall uncertainties, the utmost concern of peasant farmers in Ethiopia, could be alleviated, the risk of adopting new technologies would be greatly minimized.

There has been hardly any improvement in agricultural implements since the Agrarian Reform. Even in Arsi, where there is a Farm Implement Department under both CADU and ARDU, the dissemination of improved implements among smallholders is insignificant. A large number of peasant farmers are not aware of the availability of new farm implements from ARDU, a fact candidly admitted by ARDU in the 1982 ARDU report.

The development of improved implements at the research station has not been followed by widespread availability or adoption at the farm level. This situation reflects the lack of linkage between research and extension programs as well as the low performance of the extension services. The transmission of innovations or advice to farmers by extension agents is done haphazardly. Consequently, farmers either miss relevant information or the message is forgotten in a short period of time. This seems to be the reason why 64% of the sampled farmers in Arsi were unaware of improved farm implements. The same problem was also observed in the extension program concerned with afforestation, farm storage improvement and soil and water conservation practices.

Rural women in Ethiopia perform demanding tasks both at home and on the farm. Yet they have no access to improved and appropriate technology. And ARDU makes no distinction between the technological needs of women and those of men. The introduction of labor-saving devices in farming, food processing, water and fuel collection, transportation and other domestic activities would relieve women of some of the strenuous household work they currently perform. This would help them to increase their productivity and provide them with an opportunity to engage in income-generating activities. Such technologies could also lead to better nutrition and health since the women would have more time for child care and food preparation. Even ARDU, which has the potential to promote improved village technologies that meet the needs of Arsi women, has done hardly anything in this regard.

Ethiopia has recently faced one of the worst famine crises in its history. Although the highly-publicized starvation has been concentrated in northern Ethiopia, it has adversely affected food production in other regions of Ethiopia as well. The steady increase in population growth has not been accompanied by a growth in food production; this has resulted in a widespread chronic food crisis. In the conclusion of this study the government's reaction to the food crisis and the utility of its approach will be assessed briefly. Suggestions will be made, concerning the question of how to address these problems, based on the findings of this study.

The Ethiopian government has instituted two major emergency policies to combat hunger and attain food self-sufficiency. These are the resettlement and villagization programs. The resettlement program involves moving about 1.5 million people within a few years from the famine-stricken north to the relatively fertile regions of south and south-west Ethiopia. The program has its merits; people from nearly desert areas are moved to less populated areas of high agricultural potential. Eventually the ecologically bankrupt areas would be rehabilitated and agricultural production increased through the expansion of cultivated area. But the government's plan seems to be too ambitious. Massive resettlements are reported to be undertaken without coordinated planning at the local level; peasants are moved before appropriate areas for cultivation are identified and prepared. Consequently, settlers are faced with severe shortages of housing, social services, and farming equipment, forcing them to remain dependent upon the support of the government and local people. If the resettlement program is to be effective, settlers have to be self-supporting. This has not occurred. Thus, it is difficult to imagine how such a massive resettlement scheme, one which drains the country's finances and manpower, particularly from the Ministry of Agriculture, could significantly contribute to the attainment of urgently needed agricultural growth in the immediate future.

To be sure, resettlement from the highly-populated and ecologically degraded areas is vital to the rehabilitation of the land. But the underlying causes of the problem are bad farming practices, deforestation, soil erosion, lack of improvement in farming technology, over-cultivation, over-grazing and over-population. These problems will be best addressed when peasant institutions, particularly service cooperatives, are entrusted with the undertaking of such projects. The present approach, in which the government invests heavily in emergency projects, without an effort to involve peasant institutions in planning, is neither efficient nor effective in dealing with the roots of the problem.

As is the case in Arsi, service cooperatives could mobilize the peasantry to undertake projects central to averting the conditions that have made farming unproductive in the drought-stricken areas. And this is also the best means of utilizing the abundant labor force to attain sustainable agricultural growth in the peasant sector.

The other major government policy established in 1985 to increase food production is the villagization program. The concept of villagization was first introduced in the 1975 Rural Land Proclamation where peasant associations were encouraged to undertake it by themselves. At the moment, the government is forcing peasant associations to carry out villagization. It involves moving farmers into villages within a peasant association so that they may live in closer proximity to one another instead of in scattered homesteads. The major reason given by the government for villagization is that it will be less costly to provide peasants with social services such as schools, clinics, electricity and water if they live in villages. There is no evidence, but only a rumor, that the implicit intention of the government is to bring about collectivization.

Under the villagization policy each peasant association establishes a village. In principle, the village site is to be selected according to whether or not it can suitably provide services for farmers when they settle in the area. In practice, it is being enforced with great haste; the government takes no physical survey of the area, nor does it consult adequately with the peasant association leaders on the issue of the appropriateness of the site.

Villagization as a strategy faces several impediments to its professed goal, the attainment of agricultural growth in the short-term. First, farmers have to tear down their huts and carry the poles and other materials to construct another hut on the new site. This distracts them from their farming activities. Second, peasants will spend more time travelling from their homestead to their field. Third, the selection of the village site may be inappropriate and the farmers may then have to be relocated after only a few years, thus causing the farmers to waste valuable time and resources. Fourth, it is unlikely that the government will meet its objective to provide social services; this failure will, in turn, reduce the motivation to increase production and weaken the morale of the farmers in general.

The villagization process is very costly to the government and is disruptive to agricultural production during a period of severe food shortages. But this process can be undertaken gradually through the service cooperatives and peasant associations and conducted more smoothly at less cost when the peasants find it to be in their best interest. The merits of villagization would be more quickly understood by the peasants if the services were provided to them first. In order to increase peasant food production, it would be more appropriate to direct government resources (through the extension of services) to the peasant institutions, thereby strengthening their capacity to provide services. Then villagization could be undertaken by the service cooperatives and peasant associations at their own pace. For instance, some peasant associations have already taken communal action to control grazing land and livestock management, fuel wood, and water supply without dismantling their huts and abandoning thier homestead.

The Agrarian Reform established peasant institutions that are now an indispensable force, particularly the service cooperatives and peasant associations. It is these institutions that can best bring about urgently needed agricultural growth and direct the transformation of the rural sector. If given more autonomy by the government, these peasant institutions would be able to introduce both individual and group incentive to stimulate peasant production. Service cooperatives would serve as the primary institutions in the promotion of the cooperative movement. The essence of the cooperative movement is the generation of investable surplus through the mobilization of local resources. Such a strategy relies heavily on local resources and not on government or foreign assistance. In fact, it would enable the government to divert its limited resources to other development projects such as infrastructure, industry, and research projects that cannot be financed by the peasantry. A program based on use of service cooperatives and peasant associations is likely to contribute to the over-all development of both the rural and the urban sector.

When all is said and done, two important tasks need to be performed by policy makers and researchers, if the growth potential created by the Agrarian Reform is to be realized in the immediate term. The improvement of peasant production, the attainment of equity and the necessary social transformation will be greatly enhanced if further social research is conducted and increased autonomy of the peasant institutions are respected.

Social research that identifies and analyzes the constraints placed upon the agricultural production of peasant farmers is seriously lacking in Ethiopia. This study has generated hypotheses and identified research issues in each of the topics that merit further investigation. Through such cumulative empirical investigations, social research can assist in targeting technological information and the practical action needed to improve the well-being of farmers.

The most fundamental thing that is needed to ensure success is confidence in the peasants and the emerging peasant institutions on the part of policy-makers. The capacity of service cooperatives to undertake their own rural development projects and generate surplus through their own cooperative efforts is well demonstrated. What they need is a broader role, more independence from the government and an environment offering favorable incentives.

Peasants and peasant institutions, strengthened by the government's support and outside assistance, offer the most viable source of organized labor and suggest a strategy for attaining sustainable growth. Within these institutions collective action can be undertaken to improve production, protect the natural resources, prevent famine, and promote the cooperative movement in Ethiopia.

Notes

1. Keith Griffin and Roger Hays, "Problems of Agricultural Development in Socialist Ethiopia: An Overview and Suggested Strategy," *Journal of Peasant Studies*, Vol. 13, No. 1, October 1985, pp. 37-66. See also:
Ajit Kumar Ghose, "Transforming Feudal Agriculture: Agrarian Change in Ethiopia Since 1974," *The journal of Developing Studies*, Vol. 22, October 1985, No. 1, pp. 127-149.
2. David W. Norman, Emmy B. Simmons, and Henery M. Hays, *Farming Systems in the Nigerian Savanna: Research and Strategies for Development*, Boulder, Colorado: Westview Press, 1982. See also:
Louise O. Fresco and Susan V. Poats, "Farming System Research and Extension: An Approach to Solving Food Problems in Africa," edited by Art Hansen and Della E. Mcmillan, *Food in sub-Saharan Africa*, Boulder, Colorado: Lynne Rienner Publisher, 1986.

Appendix 1

Case Studies of Interviewed Farmers

Among the 150 farmers I have interviewed, there are a few who have meant more to me than others, for different reasons. With these farmers, my discussions have extended far beyond the questions posed in the survey questionnaire. I found their personalities, their outlook on life, and their view on the impact of the Agrarian Reform and ARDU to be revealing and pertinent to issues discussed in this study. A summary of these views is presented below.

Farmer "A " is 55 years old and has 4 children. He is hard-working, has a friendly disposition, and speaks his mind to the extent of being blunt. He lives in the Chilalo district, in the lowland zone of the Dhera Rural Development Center (RDC). He belongs to a peasant association with 164 households and a total landholding of 800 hectares. This peasant association is sparsely populated and he owns 5 ha. of land; less than he owned prior to 1975. The distance from his house to the nearest all-weather road, school, clinic, and market averages 8 kilometers.

One of the striking characteristics of Farmer A is his inquisitiveness. Once farmer A learned that I had studied and lived in the United States for a long time, he asked me numerous questions, some of which took me by surprise. For example, one of his questions was what to make of the news he hears on the radio regarding the United States. He hears that the imperialist countries, principally, the United States, presents a serious danger to world peace. At the same time, he hears that the United States is the richest country in the world. He said it is difficult for him to imagine why rich people would want to go to war.

Neither he nor his wife can read or write. His major occupation is mixed farming. He indicated that his wife participates in major farming activities, particularly animal husbandry, which accounts for a considerable part of their family income. As he put it, " without my wife I cannot see how I would be able to feed my family."

Farmer A thinks that the advice and assistance that he has received from ARDU agents has been very helpful. However, they do not come to his peasant association very frequently -- the last time that he saw an agent was 4 years ago. He was a tenant before 1975, and he welcomed the Agrarian Reform, which abolished tenancy. He feels secure about the long-term tenure of his land, and has invested in his farm recently by buying oxen. Both his agricultural output and his income have risen since 1975. He feels that ARDU contributed to these improvements, particularly by providing him with fertilizer. He is a regular credit participant, and has been using about one quintal of fertilizer every year consistently since 1975. He does not use ARDU's improved seed.

Farmer A does not like the present marketing arrangement because of the low prices that are offered him for his grain. Even after he meets the quotas set by the SC, he is not allowed to sell to private traders. He buys most of his consumer goods from private traders because they bring products (particularly agricultural equipment like ploughs and sickles) that are of good quality. He is among the 7% of farmers who reported having savings.

He chooses to remain a small holder, he says, because if he were to join a producer cooperative, others who do not work as hard as he does would take advantage of him. He is dissatisfied with the corruption and favoritism that he has seen in his service cooperative, and added that the service cooperative has not been able to account for the 11,000 Eth. birr which they collected for self-help activities. He called the executive committee of his service cooperative "the new exploiters."

The most serious problem that he faces in his farming operation is the obligation to participate in too many peasant association activities, which keep him from tending his farm as he would like to. Other major problems include the shortage of improved seed and the uncertainty of rainfall.

Farmer B is 45 years old and has six children. He is highly political -- he is a believer in socialism, and possess a clear-cut view about everything. When interviewing farmers it usually takes an average of 5 hours to complete the 20 page questionnaire. But my interview of farmer B only took an hour. His responses to the questions were well articulated and indicates a great deal of his knowledge in agriculture as well as his position on what direction he would like the Agrarian Reform to take.

Farmer B lives in the Chilalo district, in the fertile and densely populated medium altitude zone of Degaga RDC. His house is 200 meters from an all-weather road, and 5 kilometers from the nearest school and market. The peasant association to which he belongs has 319 members and a total area of 640 hectares. He owns and cultivates 2 acres.

Before 1975, Farmer B was a tenant. He supports the Agrarian Reform enthusiastically, and has served as chairman of the PA for 4 years and as a representative to the All-Ethiopian Peasant Association at the district level.

Land tenure security is not an issue that concerns him, as he plans to join a Producer Cooperative when the movement gets stronger.

Like Farmer A, he reported that both his agricultural production and his income have increased since 1975. He uses an improved harrow which he bought under CADU. He receives credit from the service cooperative, but is unhappy about the arrangement because of the delay in the delivery of fertilizer to him. But he believes that the service cooperative will overcome this problem in a short time. He uses the same amount of fertilizer as he did before 1975, and still plants the improved seed that he got under CADU. He belongs to the 4% of sampled farmers who use ARDU's improved tools.

One of the impressive aspects of Farmer B is the consistency with which he expressed his views. Farmer B does not like the present marketing arrangement, but for a different reason than the majority of the farmers, who have indicated their reasons to be the low price they receive for their agricultural produce. His reason for not liking the present marketing arrangement is that the AMC does not collect the grain from his service cooperative on time, resulting in crop losses and thereby weakening the service cooperative. He buys most of his consumer goods from the service cooperative and is satisfied with the services that it provides. He would eventually like to join a Producer Cooperative, since he believes in supporting the government's policy of promoting collective farming. His most serious problems with farming are the over-crowding in his peasant association, the delay in the delivery of fertilizer , and an excess of weeds immediately following the planting season.

Farmer C is 45 years old and has 5 children. He is a Muslim and lives in a peasant association that is located in both lowland and medium altitude zones in the Seru RDC, in the Ticho district. He is an honest man and very loyal to his polygamy, and has only one wife. He thinks polygamy is unfair to women.

He used to have 10 children, but five of them died while he lived in the lowland area. He has recently moved to the medium altitude in the same peasant association for the sake of his family. At his old home in the lowlands, he held 12 hectares, since few people lived in there. In his present situation, however, he has only 2 hectares of land; he cultivates one and uses the other for grazing.

He appreciates the advice that he has received from ARDU agents, although the last time he saw one was six years ago. At that time, he was advised of the importance of using fertilizer. Since then, he has been purchasing fertilizer (a half quintal each time) on credit. He feels that this has contributed to an increase in both his agricultural productivity and his income.

Before 1975, Farmer C was an evicted tenant, and he enthusiastically supports the Agrarian Reform program. He feels secure about his land tenure, although he has not invested in his farm since 1975. He likes the present marketing arrangement. He purchases most of his consumer goods from the service cooperatives, although he believes that private traders usually carry better quality products. With the exception of what he sees as favoritism in the distribution of goods, he is satisfied with the services provided by his service cooperative. He said that since the establishment of the cooperative shop his wife could find some of the basic items without walking long distances to the market place or nearby town.

His preference is to remain a small landholder in a peasant association, mainly because his children are very young. He fears that he would not be able to provide more financial support for them under the point system in a producer cooperative. For him, his family obligation comes first above anything else. His most serious farming problems are post-harvest losses due to pests, the threat of destruction of his crops by wild animals, and a shortage of oxen.

Farmer D is 64 years old and has 12 children, 6 of them are still dependent upon him. Yet he farms with greater vigor and tenacity than most young farmers I have observed. He is a devout Christian, one who fasts from sun-rise to sun-set during the Lent season. He came to the Arbagugu District to settle in the highland area of the Guna RDC from his original home in the Shoa province, just before the Italian invasion of Ethiopia in 1935. His house is located on a hill that over-looks cascades of hills - one more beautiful than the other. He used to farm as a tenant, but bought his own land to cultivate five years before the Agrarian Reform. He had ten hectares of land before 1975, and now owns 1.75 hectares, all of which he cultivates. His peasant association totals 134 members and covers 520 hectares of land.

His major occupation is crop farming; his most important crops are wheat and barley. Fertilizer was not available to him before ARDU began providing service to his district, but since 1976 he has been a regular credit participant, buying 1 quintal of fertilizer every year on credit. He feels secure about the long-term tenure of his land, and has invested in his farm. Both his agricultural production and his income have decreased since 1975, when the size of his farm was dramatically reduced.

Farmer D's attitude toward the present marketing arrangement is positive. He feels that the quotas of grain which he must sell to the AMC (through the SC) are fair, and after meeting this requirement he is able to find buyers for all of his excess grain. Part of the reason may be that the roads are inaccessible during the rainy season and it is difficult for the AMC to collect grain from such a remote area. He is dissatisfied with the services of his service cooperative's because it does not get him goods on time, and he prefers to buy his goods from private traders.

He has served as treasurer of his peasant association since its establishment in 1975, although he has often requested that he be replaced, as he feels that the position consumes a great deal of his time and keeps him from his farming. The general assembly of his PA has refused his request, saying that they could not find a more trustworthy person for the position.

His preference is to remain a small landholder, since he likes to cultivate his own farm. He believes that the people in his PA who want to join producer cooperatives believe that they will get government assistance if they do, but he feels that it would be a mistake to push for a producer cooperative in his area, as it is very hilly and unsuited for collective farming. The most serious problems that he faces in farming are the size of his cultivated area, delays in the delivery of fertilizer and the destruction of some of his crops by animals like chimps and wild pigs.

In all, the qualities of these farmers I have observed such as the inquisitiveness and the desire to learn of farmer A, the consistency and decisiveness of farmer B, the loyalty to the his family and fairness of farmer C, and the sincerity and commitment to improve his own as well as his community's welfare of farmer D leads me to believe that the a development strategy lead by peasants and peasant institutions could be a viable reality given adequate and appropriate support from the government and outside sources.

Index to Names and Places

Subject Index

P-6x